GENEALOGY

OF

WILLIAM CARVER

FROM

HERTFORDSHIRE, ENGLAND

IN

1682

BY

ELIAS CARVER
ATTORNEY-AT-LAW
OF DOYLESTOWN, PA.

1903

To my son, HENRY CARVER, a graduate of Yale University of Class 1883, and of the Law Department of the University of Pennsylvania of Class 1886, and now practicing law in the City of Philadelphia, Pennsylvania, this work is respectfully dedicated.

WILLIAM CARVER

John Carver and Mary Lane, his wife, came from Hartford, England, with William Penn, in the ship "Welcome," of three hundred tons burden; Robert Greenaway was master. One hundred persons, it is said, embarked September 11, 1682, at Deal, England, and arrived in the river Delaware the 28th day of the 8th month, 1682 (old style). Ninety-five of the one hundred persons who embarked have been accounted for. There is another person by the name of Roland, whose name appears in a little book in the Register's Office at Doylestown, making ninety-six.

Joseph Carver, Jacob Carver, and William Carver came in the ship "Samson," about the same time.

They were all members of the religious Society of Friends and settled in Byberry, Philadelphia County, Pennsylvania. They took up a tract of land there and dug a cave in which they lived until they built a house.

The old farm remained in the family, and in the name of John Carver, for five successive generations.

Joseph Carver married and moved to North Carolina, near Carver's Creek. Jacob died unmarried.

William Carver, the first of our American ancestry, married 11th month 14, 1689 (old style), at Middletown Monthly Meeting of Friends, Bucks County, Pennsylvania, Joan Kinsey, a descendant of Chief Justice Kinsey (see Middletown Monthly Meeting of Friends' Minutes). She having died, he, in 1723, married at Falls, Bucks County, Pennsylvania, Grace Carter (see Minutes of Falls Monthly Meeting), a widow, whose maiden name was Paxson, from Bristol, England (see Will Book No. 1, page 44, at Doylestown). He had one child by her, named Hannah. William Carver died at Byberry, Philadelphia County, in May, 1736. His will is recorded at Philadelphia, in Will Book E, page 369, June 2, 1736. Grace Carver, his widow, died in 1737. Her will is recorded at Philadelphia, in Will Book F, page 42, in 1737. She left the most of her estate to her son, Robert Carter.

William Carver, a son of the first William and Joan, his wife, married in 1719, Elizabeth Walmsley, a daughter of Henry Walmsley and Mary Searle, his wife, who was a daugnter of Francis Searle. Henry Walmsley was the younger son of Thomas Walmsley and Elizabeth, his wife, who came from Yorkshire, England, in the ship "Welcome," with William Penn, in 1682.

Thomas Walmsley and Mary, his wife, by their Indenture, dated December 16, 1735, and recorded in Deed Book No. 184, page 308, conveyed to the said William Carver, 235 acres and 22 perches of land in Buckingham Township, Bucks County, Pennsylvania, a little way easterly from Forest Grove. He was the first Carver who settled in Bucks County. He died in Buckingham Township, in January, 1759. His will is recorded at Doylestown, in Will Book No. 2, page 353, January 30, 1759. His widow, Elizabeth, died in Warwick Township, Bucks County, Pennsylvania, in February, 1772.

The family has a Coat of Arms and a Motto: *Conjunctio firmat*—"union strengthens."

PLAN OF THE BOOK

Each of the children of William Carver[1] will be found at the head of one of the branches of the family tree.

The generation to which each person belongs will be known by the small figure on the right of a name.

At a marriage the number is put in parenthesis ( ) for distinction.

Successive generations will be understood by the given names with their generations as found in the book, which read from right to left, as follows:

(Joseph[3], William[2], William[1].)

KEY TO ABBREVIATIONS

A small b. for born; d. for died; m. for married; unm. for unmarried; mo. for month.

FOR DATES

1754, 12 mo. 15, is December 15, 1754; the first figure for the month.

GENEALOGY
OF
WILLIAM CARVER

William Carver[1] was born in England and came into Byberry, Philadelphia, Pa., in 1682. In the 11th month, 1689 (old style), he married at Friends' Meeting, Middletown Twp, Bucks Co., Pa., Joan Kinsey, a descendant of Chief Justice Kinsey. This wife having died, he married at Falls Monthly Meeting, in 1723, Grace Carter, his second wife, a widow, whose maiden name was Paxson, from Bristol, England. By her he had but one child, Hannah. He died at Byberry, in May, 1736, and she in 1737. His will was proven, June 2, 1736, and recorded in Philadelphia in Will Book E, page 369; his widow's in Will Book F, page 42, in 1737. His children are, as shown by his will:

1. Sarah Carver, b. 1690, 10 mo. 20, m. —— Marshall.
2. Rachel Carver, m. —— Denkon, or Demkon.
3. William Carver, b. 1694, 3 mo. 22.
4. Rebecca Carver, m. —— Brock.
5. Hester Carver, m. —— Knight.
6. Mary Carver, m. Samuel Worthington.
7. Hannah Carver—by his second wife.

(William[2], William[1].)

(3.) William Carver, Jr.[2]—a son of William and Joan Kinsey, his wife—was born in Byberry, Philadelphia, Pa., 1694, 3 mo. 22; married 1719, 10 mo. 28, Elizabeth Walmsley, daughter of Henry and Mary Searle, his wife. In 1735–6, he moved to Buckingham Twp, Bucks Co., Pa., to the farm he purchased of Thomas Walmsley. He was the first Carver who settled in Bucks Co. He died there in January, 1759. His widow died in Warwick Twp, in 1772. His will was recorded at Doylestown, Pa., in Will Book No. 2, page 353, January 30, 1759; his widow's in Will Book No. 3, page 258, March 2, 1772. His sons, William and Henry, were his executors. His children are:

8. William Carver.
9. Joseph Carver.
10. Henry Carver.
11. Elizabeth Carver, m. Thomas Buckman.
12. Mary Carver, m. Josiah Wilkinson.
13. Rebecca Carver, m. Thomas Schofield.
14. Martha Carver, m. Isaac Worthington.

(William[2], William[1].)

(8.) William Carver[3]—a son of William Carver and Elizabeth Walmsley, his wife—was born in Buckingham Twp, Bucks Co., Pa.; married Sarah Strickland, in 1755, 6 month, and died 1803, 9 month 27. His will is dated September 17, 1803, and recorded in Will Book No. 6, page 500, October 15, 1803. His executors were his sons, William and Joseph. He left a widow and the following children:

15. William Carver.
16. Joseph Carver.
17. Elizabeth Carver,   m. David Bradshaw, 1779, 12 mo. 1.
18. Mary Carver, b. 1764, 5 mo. 4, m. John Kirk.

(William[2], William[1].)

(9.) Joseph Carver[3]—another son of William Carver and Elizabeth Walmsley, his wife—was twice married, as his will shows, but the name of his first wife is not known, nor when he was married to her. His children must be by her.

In 1776, 11 month 20, he married his second wife, Hannah Worthington, daughter of John of Byberry. He resided in Buckingham Twp. His will bears date 1790, 12 month 9, and recorded in Will Book No. 6, page 58, November 9, 1797. He left no widow. His children are:

19. Joseph Carver.
20. Joel Carver.
21. John Carver,
22. Ruth Carver,   m. John Terry, Esq.
23. Martha Carver,   m. Smith Price.
24. Rachel Carver,   m. —— Tomlinson.
25. William Carver, b. 1746, 3 mo. 29.

His sons, William and Joseph, were his executors.

(William[2], William[1].)

(10.) Henry Carver,[3]—another son of William Carver and Elizabeth Walmsley, his wife—married Rachel Smith, daughter of William and Rebecca Wilson of Wrightstown Twp, Bucks Co., Pa., in 1755. He died in Buckingham Twp, in October, 1774. His will is dated September 10, 1774, and recorded in Will Book No. 3, page 375, October 25, 1774. His executors were his wife, Rachel, and his brothers, Joseph and William, his sons being minors. The following are his children:

26. Elizabeth Carver, b. 1756.
27. Rachel Carver, b. 5 mo. 10, 1758.
28. Thomas Carver, b. 1761.
29. John Carver, b. 1762.

WILLIAM CARVER

30. Joseph Carver, b. 10 mo. 3, 1765.
31. Benjamin Carver, b. 1767.

Rachel, his widow, married 1779, 11th month 10, her second husband, Samuel Harrold from Ireland, a descendant of Samuel Harrold of Normandy, France. He was a merchant and became wealthy, owning land in both Pennsylvania and Virginia. He died the forepart of November, 1803. His will bears date 1803, 5th month 26, and is recorded in Will Book No. 6, page 504, November 10, 1803. He died in Buckingham Twp, Bucks Co., Pa.

Samuel was born in Cavin County, Ireland, in 1728; came to America at the age of 17, and married a lady by the name of Russell, by whom he had five sons and two daughters. Their names are: William Harrold, James, Samuel, Joseph, John, Sarah and Elizabeth.

Samuel Harrold and Rachel Carver, his second wife, had two children, viz.:

32. David Harrold, b. 1780, 12 mo.
33. Rebecca Harrold, b. 1783, 3 mo. 19.

Rachel, his widow, died in June, 1824. Her will is recorded in Will Book No. 10, page 297, June 18, 1824.

(William[2], William[1].)

(11.) Elizabeth Carver[3]—a daughter of William Carver and Elizabeth Walmsley, his wife—married Thomas Buckman in December 11, 1753. He was born at Newtown, Bucks Co., Pa., 1729, 4th month 12, and died there about April 1, 1804. She survived him. They had no children. (For some reason they separated.) He states in his will, which is dated July 5, 1799, and recorded in Will Book No. 6, page 559, April 9, 1804 (and is now free for the public), that "he had three children by Mary "Wisener, the woman who now and has for many years last past lived "with me in the place of a wife." Their names are "Thomas Buckman, "Mary Buckman and Stacy Buckman." Major Thomas Buckman, the son of Thomas and Mary Wisener, was the father of Monroe Buckman of Doylestown, Pa.

(William[2], William[1].)

(12.) Mary Carver[3]—another daughter of William and Elizabeth Walmsley, his wife—married Josiah Wilkinson, son of John and Mary Walker, his wife. Their children are:

34. William Wilkinson, b. 1753, 11 mo. 27.
35. Elizabeth Wilkinson, b. 1755, 2 mo. 14.
36. John Wilkinson, b. 1763, 12 mo 18.
37. Joseph Wilkinson, b. 1766, 6 mo. 13.
38. Thomas Wilkinson, b. 1769, 2 mo. 26.
39. Asa Wilkinson, b. 1772, 4 mo. 22.

The family moved to Chester Co., Pa.

GENEALOGY OF

(William[2], William[1].)

(13.) Rebecca Carver[3]—another daughter of William Carver and Elizabeth Walmsley, his wife—married at Friends' Meeting, Buckingham, 1755, 12th month, Thomas Schofield. In 1763, 12th month 5, they moved to Providence, Chester Co., Pa. They had three children.

(William[2], William[1].)

(14.) Martha Carver[3]—another daughter of William Carver and Elizabeth Walmsley, his wife—married 1760, 11th month 22, Isaac Worthington. They moved to Chester Co., Pa. He died there 1800, 11th month 12, leaving his wife surviving. Their children are:

40. William Worthington.
41. Amos Worthington.
42. Heber Worthington.
43. Joseph Worthington.
44. John Worthington.
45. Elizabeth Worthington.
46. Mary Worthington.

(William[3], William[2], William[1].)

(15.) William Carver[4]—a son of William Carver and Sarah Strickland, his wife—married Phebe Worthington, 1783, 4th month, out of Friends' Meeting, and died in Buckingham Twp in June, 1838. His will is dated May 4, 1838, and recorded in Will Book No. 11, page 538, June 21, 1838. He left a widow and children:

47. Israel Carver, b. 1791.
48. David P. Carver.
49. Miles Carver.
50. Ann Carver.
51. Major Henry Carver.
52. Joseph Carver, b. 1788, 2 mo. 10.
53. James Carver, b. 1796, 2 mo. 21.
54. Sarah Carver, b. 1794, 2 mo. 19.
55. Benjamin Carver, b. 1799, 10 mo. 8.

His sons, Israel, David and Miles were his executors.

(William[3], William[2], William[1].)

(16.) Joseph Carver[4]—another son of William Carver and Sarah Strickland, his wife—married Elizabeth Kimble. He died in December, 1835. His will is dated October 1, 1828, and a codicil dated April 1, 1834. They are recorded in Will Book No. 11, page 373, December 17, 1835. He left a widow and the following children:

WILLIAM CARVER

56. Sarah Carver, b. May 8, 1785, d. young.
57. William Carver, b. May 5, 1787, d. young.
58. Anthony Carver, b. January 4, 1789, d. young.
59. Esther Carver, b. May 5, 1790.
60. Joseph Carver, Esq., b. June 22, 1792.
61. Miles Carver, b. August 30, 1793, d. young.
62. Jesse P. Carver, b. April 7, 1798.
63. Eliza Carver, b. April 30, 1801; m. Samuel Kirk.

(William[3], William[2], William.[1])

(17.) Elizabeth Carver[4]—a daughter of William Carver and Sarah Strickland, his wife—married David Bradshaw, of Buckingham Twp, a weaver by occupation, in 1779, 12th month 1. He died in February, 1828. His wife died before him, leaving children:

64. Sarah Bradshaw, b. 1780, 9 mo. 29.
65. William Bradshaw, b. 1782, 6 mo. 8.
66. Sidney Bradshaw, b. 1784, 4 mo. 10.
67. David Bradshaw, b. 1786, 4 mo. 21.
68. Ruth Bradshaw, b. 1789, 9 mo. 12.
69. James Bradshaw, b. 1791, 6 mo. 15.
70. Elizabeth Bradshaw, b. 1799, 6 mo. 25.

(William[3], William[2], William[1].)

(18.) Mary Carver[4]—another daughter of William Carver and Sarah Strickland, his wife—was born 1764, 5th month 4; married John Kirk of Buckingham Twp, and died in 1857, 1st month 24. He died intestate May 1, 1815, leaving widow and children:

71. William Kirk, b. 1787, 11 mo. 15.
72. Sarah Kirk, b. 1790, 12 mo. 2.
73. Mary Kirk, b. 1792, 5 mo. 5.
74. John Kirk, b. 1795, 8 mo. 26.
75. Isaac C. Kirk, b. 1797, 6 mo. 11.
76. Stephen Kirk, b. 1800, 1 mo. 8.

William Kirk of Buckingham, whose will is dated 1817, 1st month 18, and proven November 2, 1821, in Will Book No. 10, page 50, was the father of the said John Kirk who married Mary Carver, and also of Sarah, wife of Benjamin Carver.

(Joseph[3], William[2], William[1].)

(19.) Joseph Carver[4]—a son of Joseph Carver and ———, his wife, of Solebury Twp—married Mary Van Sant. He died in May, 1819. His will is dated 1818, 5th month 6, and recorded in Will Book No. 9, page 328, May 14, 1819. He left a widow and children:

77. Cornelius Carver.
78. Garret V. Carver.
79. Joseph E. Carver, died in July, 1855, by his own hands.
80. Mary V. Carver, b. 1785, 7 mo. 7; d. 1836, 8 mo. 15.
81. Martha Carver, m. John Fretz; no children.
82. Joel Carver, b. 1798, 3 mo. 5; d. 1881, 9 mo. 2.

(Joseph[3], William[2], William[1].)

(20) Joel Carver[4]—another son of Joseph Carver and wife—married Ann Smith in 1776, 11th month 26. He died in Northampton Twp, Bucks Co., Pa., March 1816. His will is dated January 27, 1816, and recorded in Will Book No. 9, page 90. He left a widow and children:

83. Joseph Carver, b. 1777.
84. Robert Carver.
85. Ann Carver, b. 1786, 4 mo. 14; m. Abraham Lloyd.
86. Joel Carver.
87. Rachel Carver, d. unm., in June, 1829.
88. Martha Carver, d. unm., September 1, 1850.
89. Hannah Carver, m. first George Hobensack, second Thomas Willard.

(Joseph[3], William[2], William[1].)

(21.) John Carver—another son of Joseph Carver and wife—married at Sweed's Church, September 23, 1778, Ann Carver, who was born 1757, 4th month 6, of Isaac Carver and Phebe Walmsley, whose parents were Mary Paxson and Thomas Walmsley. He lived in Buckingham Twp, and died leaving a widow and children:

90. Joseph Carver.
91. Isaac Carver.
92. Eli Carver.
93. John Carver.
94. Levi Carver, d. without issue.
95. Miller D. Carver, d. childless.
96. Amos Carver, d. childless.
97. Miles Carver.
98. Martha Carver.
99. Phebe Carver, b. 1787, 11 mo. 10, on Saturday.
100. Mary Carver.
101. Amy Carver, b. 1790, 7 mo. 30.
102. Ann Carver, b. 1795, 3 mo. 10.

WILLIAM CARVER

(Joseph³, William², William¹.)

(22.) Ruth Carver⁴—a daughter of Joseph Carver and wife—married John Terry, Esq., of Wrightstown Twp, son of John Terry, who died in 1790. Letters of administration to Esq. Terry's estate were granted to his son Joseph Carver Terry, December 7, 1829.

At February term of Court, 1830, Charles Thompson petitioned the Court for a citation, citing Joseph C. Terry to increase his security.

John Terry, Esq., was twice married. The first three children named were by Ruth Carver Terry, his second wife. The other four were by his first wife:

103. Joseph C. Terry, b. 1792.
104. Martha Terry, b. 1795.
105. James Terry, b. 1797.

Ruth Carver had a natural son named Jacob.

(Joseph³, William², William¹.)

(23.) Martha Carver—another daughter of Joseph Carver and first wife—married Smith Price of Plumstead. They had one child:

105½. John Price, Esq.

She died and Smith married Hannah Jones, and had children: Mary, Burroughs, Jonathan, Joseph, Samuel and Smith Price, M.D. Smith Price, the father, died in October, 1816.

(Joseph³, William², William¹.)

(24.) Rachel Carver⁴—another daughter of Joseph Carver and his first wife—married —— Tomlinson.

(Joseph³, William², William¹.)

(25.) William Carver⁴—another son of Joseph Carver and his first wife—was born in Buckingham Twp, 1746, 3d month 29; married Martha Addis, who was born 1752, 3d month 3. William died in Solesbury Twp in the spring of 1814, intestate. John Blackfan administered to his estate. At May term of court, 1814, he petitioned for an inquest. William left a widow and children, to wit:

106. Ann Carver, b. 1777, 1 mo. 22, d. Aug. 24, 1778.
107. Martha Carver, b. 1778, 11 mo. 15.
108. John Carver, b. 1780, 10 mo. 15; killed in the war of 1812, unmarried.
109. Elizabeth Carver, b. 1783, 4 mo. 10.
110. Joseph Carver, b. 1785, 4 mo. 18; called "Fifing Joe;" was not married.
111. Hannah Carver, b. 1787, 9 mo. 10.
112. William Carver, b. 1789, 10 mo. 25, d. 1793, 7 mo. 18.
113. Izri Carver, b. 1792, 9 mo. 6.

John Carver and Fifing Joe were both in the war of 1812. Fifing Joe played magnificently on the fife. He saw his brother John shot by his side; he was killed.

(Henry[3], William[2], William[1].)

(26.) Elizabeth Carver[4]—a daughter of Henry Carver and Rachel Smith, his wife—was born in Buckingham Twp, in 1756; married 1791, 10th month 12, Aaron Oldden of Middlesex Co., N. J. They had children:

114. Giles Oldden.
115. Catharine Oldden.
116. Rachel Oldden.

Her husband died and she married for her second husband Anthony Fretz, but they had no children.

(Henry[3], William[2], William[1].)

(27.) Rachel Carver[4]—also a daughter of Henry Carver and Rachel Smith, his wife—was born in Buckingham Twp, 1758, 5th month 10; married Jesse Ely, a son of Hugh, 1791, 10th month 12, and died in Carversville, Bucks Co., Pa., in October, 1829. Her will is dated 1829, 10th month 8, and recorded in Will Book No. 10, page 751, November 14, 1829. Their children are:

117. Hugh B. Ely, b. 1792, 11 mo. 3.
118. Charles Ely, b. 1794, 6 mo. 24, d. unm.
119. Joseph O. Ely, b. 1797, 6 mo. 14, d. young.
120. William C. Ely, b. 1801, 3 mo. 17.
121. Alfred Ely, b. 1809, 10 mo. 11, d. young.
122. Henry C. Ely, b. 1811, 10 mo. 8.
123. Alfred Ely [second], b. 1813, 7 mo. 27, d. young.
124. Joseph Ely [second], b. 1814, 8 mo. 30, d. young.

(Henry[3], (William[2], William[1].)

(28.) Thomas Carver[4]—a son of Henry Carver and Rachel Smith, his wife—was born in Buckingham Twp, Bucks Co., Pa., in 1761. He married 1782, 6th month 12, Sarah Harrold, daughter of Samuel by his first wife Russel, and died intestate in the fall of 1804. He owned the hotel property at Bushington, in Buckingham Twp. His brother, Joseph Carver, and his brother-in-law, Jesse Ely, were his administrators. They sold his real estate for the payment of debts. Elisha Wilkinson bought 104 acres of it situate in Buckingham Twp, and the deed was made in the spring of 1805. His children are:

125. Samuel Carver, M.D.
126. David Carver.
127. Henry Carver.
128. Elizabeth H. Carver.
129. James Carver.

WILLIAM CARVER

(Henry[3], William[2], William[1].)

(29.) John Carver[4]—another son of Henry Carver and Rachel Smith, his wife—was born in Buckingham in 1762. On the second day of June he married Sarah Ellicott, a daughter of Thomas and Ann Ely, his wife. He died intestate in Plumstead Twp in February, 1821. His admistrators were John Price, Esq., and Nicholas Swartz. He had nine children, to wit:

130. Rachel Carver, b. 1785, 12 mo. 25.
131. Thomas Carver, b. 1787, 4 mo. 23.
132. Pamelia Carver, b. 1792, 5 mo. 22.
133. Ann Carver, b. 1794, 11 mo. 21.
134. Sarah Ann Carver, b. 1799, 3 mo. 2.
135. Letitia Ellicott Carver, b. 1802, 12 mo. 9.
136. John Ellicott Carver, b. 1805, 11 mo. 7.
137. Rebecca Gillingham Carver, b. 1809, 8 mo. 6.
138. Henry Ellicott Carver, b. 1815, 3 mo. 13.

(Henry[3], William[2], William[1].)

(30.) Joseph Carver[4]—another son of Henry Carver and Rachel Smith, his wife—born 1765, 10th month 3. In the spring of 1788 he married Hannah Carey, who was born 1769, 4th month 29. She was a daughter of Thomas Carey of Plumstead Twp. Thomas was the son of John Carey, who died in Plumstead in 1792. His will is dated 1760, 9th month 14, and is recorded in Will Book No. 5, page 302, August 9, 1792. He left a widow, Elizabeth, and children: John Carey, Thomas Carey, Elizabeth Carey, Ann Carey, Mary Carey, Hannah Carey, Elias Carey and Samuel Carey.

Thomas, in 1763, 10th month 6, married Mary Skelton, whose maiden name was Townsend, a widow of Joseph Skelton, who died intestate in April, 1762, leaving children. Joseph Skelton, who lay in bed for twenty years pretending that he was not able to get up. John Skelton, wheelwright, married Sarah Kimble, 1777, 3d month 26. Mary Skelton married Joseph White, a tailor, and Sarah Skelton married John Shaw of Plumstead as per Deed Book No. 24, page 469. He died and she then married Joseph Stradling of Plumstead. Thomas Carey's will bears date 1806, 12th month 24, and recorded in Will Book No. 8, page 7, December, 1808. He survived his wife and left children: Thomas Carey; Elizabeth Carey married Isaac Pickering, and Hannah Carey married Joseph Carver. After the marriage of Joseph Carver and Hannah Carey they resided in Plumstead Twp, where most of their children were born. He and his brother-in-law, Jesse Ely, bought of the executors of Thomas Ellicott, by deed dated 1799, 4th month 1,

10 GENEALOGY OF

and recorded in Deed Book No. 61, page 285, 80¾ acres of land situtate in Solesbury Twp, at Milton, now called Carversville. Jesse Ely and Rachel, his wife, by deed of release, dated April 10, 1804, conveyed and released to the said Joseph Carver 31 acres of the 80¾, with a grist mill, saw mill and other buildings upon it. Joseph moved upon the property and died there January 4, 1836, æt. 70 years, 3 months, 1 day. His will is dated November 20, 1835, and recorded in Will Book No. 11, page 388, January 29, 1836. His widow, Hannah, died in Buckingham, 1842, 10th month 22, intestate. Her son, Eli, administered to her estate. They had the following named children:

139. Thomas Carver, b. 1788, 9 mo. 9.
140. Henry Carver, b. 1790, 2 mo. 8.
141. Rachel Carver, b. 1794, 8 mo. 24.
142. Mary Carver, b. 1798, 2 mo. 26.
143. Anne Carver, b. 1802, 1 mo. 26.
144. Eli Carver, b. 1804, 6 mo. 4.
145. Julia H. Carver, b. 1809, 9 mo. 28.

(Henry[3], William[2], William[1].)

(31.) Benjamin Carver[4]—another son of Henry Carver and Rachel Smith, his wife—was born in Buckingham Twp, Bucks Co., Pa., in 1767. He married, in 1789, Sarah Kirk, daughter of William, whose will was proven November 2, 1821, in Will Book No. 10, page 50. William was the father of John Kirk, who married Mary Carver (see No. 25). Benjamin died intestate, January 4, 1837, leaving his second wife, Ann. His wife, Sarah, died 1816, 10th month 14. His children are:

146. Amos Carver, b. 1791, 5 mo. 22.
147. William Carver, b. 1793, 3 mo. 6.
148. Jesse Carver, b. 1797, 3 mo. 24.
149. Cynthia Carver, b. 1800, 8 mo. 19.
150. Rachel Carver, b. 1802, 12 mo. 3.
151. Levi Carver, b. 1805, 6 mo. 12.
152. Isaac Carver, b. 1808, 1 mo. 6.
153. Miranda Carver, b. 1810, 10 mo. 25.
154. Mary Carver, b. 1813, 5 mo. 29.
155. Stephen Carver, b. 1816, 10 mo. 14, d. the next day.
156. Elizabeth Carver, b. 1795, 10 mo. 3.

(Rachel[3], William[2], William[1].)

(32.) David Harrold[4]—a son of Samuel Harrold and Rachel Carver, his second wife, who was the widow of Henry Carver, deceased—was born in Buckingham Twp, December 12, 1780. He married Martha Wall, daughter of George of Solesbury, 1811, 7th month 9. He filled the office of Associate Judge three different times in Madison Co., Ohio, and died at the Harrold Homestead, in said county, 1862, 5th month 13. The following are his children:

157. Charles Harrold, b. 1813, 12 mo. 22.
158. Alfred Harrold, b. 1815, 5 mo. 11, d. August, 1836.
159. William Harrold, b. 1818, 11 mo. 19.
160. Soland Harrold, died in infancy.
161. Caroline Harrold, died in infancy.

(Rachel[3], William[2], William[1].)

(33.) Rebecca Harrold[4]—a daughter of Samuel Harrold and Rachel Smith Carver, his second wife, and widow of Henry Carver, deceased—was born in Buckingham Twp, Pa., 1783, 3d month 19. She and Joseph Gillingham were married at Friends' Meeting, Buckingham, 1802, 4th month 14. She died in Philadelphia, 1871, 3d month 10, æt. 88 years, less 8 days. They had children:

162. Rachel H. Gillingham, b. 1803, 4 mo., d. in infancy.
163. Samuel H. Gillingham, b. 1804, 5 mo. 31.
164. Mary Anna Gillingham, b. 1806, 7 mo., d. in infancy.
165. Ann Gillingham, b. 1807, 12 mo. 5.
166. Emmaline L. Gillingham, b. 1809, 11 mo. 11.
167. Elizabeth Gillingham, b. 1811, 12 mo. 10.
168. Rebecca Gillingham, b. 1813, 11 mo. 12; unm.
169. Josephine Gillingham, b. 1816, 3 mo. 3, d. in infancy.
170. Joseph H. Gillingham, b. 1818, 8 mo. 18; unm.
171. Catharine Oldden Gillingham, b. 1820, 11 mo. 20; unm.
172. Frances Gillingham, b. 1823, 7 mo. 2; unm.
173. Caroline Gillingham, b. 1825, 9 mo. 17; unm.

Joseph Gillingham, the father, was born of Yoemans Gillingham and Bridget Moon, his wife, 1780, 8th month 3, in Bucks Co., Pa., and died May 3, 1867, æt. 86 years, 9 months.

(William[4], William[2], William[1].)

(47.) Israel Carver[5]—a son of William Carver and Phebe Worthington, his wife—was born in Buckingham in 1791; married Charity ———, and died intestate at Quakertown, Bucks Co., Pa., in January, 1871. His wife died 1852, 6th month 30. His children are:

174. Frank Morris Carver.
175. Sarah Carver.
176. William Carver.
177. David Carver.
178. Deborah E. Carver, b. 1835, 9 mo. 24.
179. Mary Carver.
180. Strickland Carver.
181. Lydia Carver.

(48.) David P. Carver, of Buckingham—another son of William Carver and Phebe Worthington, his wife—married Rachel Martendale, and died intestate in the fall of 1841. His children are:

182. Jane G. Carver.
183. Evelina P. Carver.
184. Theodore Carver.
185. Stephen Carver.

(William[4], William[3], William[2], William[1].)

(49.) Miles Carver[5], of Buckingham—another son of William Carver and Phebe Worthington, his wife—married Ann Martendale, and died May 1, 1877. His children are:

186. Beulah Carver.
187. Mary Carver.
188. Benjamin Watson Carver.
189. T. Ellwood Carver.
190. Angelina Carver.
191. George W. Carver.

(William[4], William[3], William[2], William[1].)

(50.) Ann Carver[5]—a daughter of William Carver and Phebe Worthington, his wife—was born in Buckingham; married Samuel McDowell, and died. Her children are:

192. James McDowell.
193. Napoleon McDowell; d. unm.
194. Martha McDowell.

(William[4], William[3], William[2], William[1].)

(51.) Major Henry Carver[5]—another son of William Carver and Phebe Worthington, his wife—was born in Buckingham. He was twice married: first, to Catharine Worthington; second, to ———, by whom he had one child. He died at Point Pleasant on the Atlantic Coast in New Jersey. His children are:

195. William Carver, d. um.
196. Henry Carver.
197. Margaret Carver.
198. Thomas Early Carver.
199. Willets Carver, d. young.
200. Caroline Carver.
201. Nelson Carver, d. young.
202. Ann Eliza Carver.
203. John Carver.
204. Charles Carver, d. young.
205. Mary Carver.
206. Kate Carver.
207. George W. Carver, by his second wife.

WILLIAM CARVER

(William[4], William[3], William[2], William[1].)

(52.) Joseph Carver[5]—another son of William Carver and Phebe Worthington, his wife—was born in Buckingham, 1788, 2d month 10. He married, 1818, 2d month 19, Rebecca White, daughter of Amos and Ann Beans, his wife. Ann was a daughter of Matthew Beans and Margery Paxson, his wife. Rebecca was born 1800, 5th month 21, and died 1877, 2d month 18. Joseph died 1857, 4th month 22. His children are:

208. Maria Carver, b. 1819, 5 mo. 24.
209. Eli W. Carver, b. 1821, 5 mo. 25.
210. Benjamin Carver, b. 1823, 8 mo. 12.
211. Aaron E. Carver, b. 1825, 9 mo. 19.
212. George W. Carver, b. 1827, 12 mo. 11.
213. Stephen P. Carver, b. 1829, 11 mo. 21.
214. Albert W. Carver, b. 1831, 12 mo. 13.
215. Phebe Ann Carver, b. 1833, 11 mo. 11.
216. Rachel Carver, b. 1835, 10 mo. 27.
217. William Carver, b. 1837, 9 mo. 19.
218. Harrison W. Carver, b. 1842, 7 mo. 12.

(53.) James Carver—another son of William Carver and Phebe Worthington, his wife—was born in Buckingham, 1796, 2d month 21. He was twice married: first, to Mary Paxson, daughter of Samuel Paxson—they had four children; secondly, to Tamor Monday—they had twelve children. Tamor died in Plumstead, 1882, 7th month 14, æt. 76 years, 4 months, 14 days. James died in Plumstead 1882, 12th month 19, æt. 86 years, 9 months, 27 days. His children are:

219. Alfred S. Carver, b. 1820.
220. Paxson Carver, b. 1822, 4 mo. 11.
221. Harriet Carver.
222. Miles Carver, d. in infancy.
223. Edwin Carver, by second wife.
224. Mary Carver, by second wife.
225. Hannah Carver, by second wife.
226. Phebe Carver, by second wife.
227. Nathan Carver, by second wife.
228. Henry Carver, by second wife.
229. Eugene Carver, by second wife.
230. Frank Carver, by second wife.
231. Charles Carver, by second wife, d. unm.
232. Margaret Carver, by second wife.
233. Kate Carver, by second wife, d. unm.
234. Amanda Carver, by second wife.

GENEALOGY OF

(William[4], William[3], William[2], William[1].)

(54.) Sarah Carver[5]—another daughter of William Carver and Phebe Worthington, his wife—was born 1794, 2d month, 19; married William Stradling, 1818, 10th month 22, and died leaving her husband surviving. Her children are:

235. Smith Stradling, b. 1820, 4 mo. 23.
236. Mary Stradling, b. 1821, 8 mo. 25.
237. Hutchinson Stradling, b. 1823, 2 mo. 17.
238. Miles Stradling, b. 1824, 10 mo. 24, d. young.
239. Martha B. Stradling, b. 1828, 8 mo. 12.

(William[4], William[3], William[2], William[1].)

(55.) Benjamin Carver[5]—another son of William Carver and Phebe Worthington, his wife—was born in Buckingham, 1799, 10th month 8; married Hannah Robinson, 1822, 12th month 12, and died 1842, 5th month 4. His children are:

240. Nathan Carver, b. 1823, 11 mo. 27, d. 1846, 7 mo. 13, unm.
241. Miles Carver, b. 1828, 10 mo. 19, d. 1831 9 mo. 10, unm.
241½. Martha B. Carver, b. 1836, 5 mo. 20.
242. Smith Carver, b. 1839, 2 mo. 19.
243. Benjamin Carver, b. 1842, 2 mo. 4.

(Joseph[4], William[3], William[2], William[1].)

(59.) Esther Carver—a daughter of Joseph Carver and Elizabeth Kimble, his wife—was twice married: first, to William McDowell—he died 1818, 12th month 6, in his 31st year; secondly, to Mahlon Blaker, 1823, 1st month 29. Esther died 1851, 3d month 3, æt. 60 years, 9 months, 28 days; and Mahlon, 1857, 1st month 26. Her children are:

244. Eliza Ann McDowell, b. 1811, 4 mo. 10.
245. Hannah McDowell.
246. George McDowell.
247. Joseph McDowell.
248. William McDowell, b. 1818, 12 mo. 18. } Twins.
249. Robert McDowell, b. 1818, 12 mo. 18. }
250. Charles M. Blacker, by second husband, b. 1824, 8 mo. 12.

At an Orphans' Court, held in March, 1819, Robert McDowell and Joseph Carver, the paternal and maternal grandparents, were appointed guardians for the children, the eldest being seven years old.

WILLIAM CARVER

(Joseph⁴, William³, William², William¹.)

(60.) Joseph Carver, Esq.—a son of Joseph Carver and Elizabeth Kimble, his wife—was born in Buckingham, 1792, 5th month 22; married Cynthia Kirk, daughter of William, in 1815. She died in 1861, 11th month 6; and he in 1870, 4th month 8. Joseph was a Justice of the Peace for many years and Register for three years. Their children are:

251. William K. Carver, b. 1816, 5 mo. 25.
252. Wilson J. Carver, b. 1818.
253. Jesse Carver, b. 1820.
254. Joseph Carver, Jr., b. 1822, 6 mo. 9.
255. Mary E. Carver, b. 1825, 9 mo. 9.
256. Elizabeth K. Carver, b. 1828, 3 mo. 13.

(Joseph⁴, William³, William², William¹.)

(62.) Jesse P. Carver⁵—another son of Joseph Carver and Elizabeth Kimble, his wife—was born in Buckingham, 1798, 4th month 7; married Elizabeth Tucker. He died at Pineville, in Wrightstown Twp in 1883, 8th month 13. His children are:

257. C. Harrison Carver.
258. Lewis T. Carver.
259. John J. Carver. He died at the Insane Hospital at Harrisburg, about September 5, 1881.

(Joseph⁴, William³, William², William¹.)

(63.) Eliza Carver⁵—a daughter of Joseph Carver and Elizabeth Kimble, his wife—was born in Buckingham Twp, 1801, 4th month 30. She married Samuel Kirk; had no children living; died 1828, 10th month 20, in her 27th year. She had an infant son that died October 25, 1828.

(Elizabeth⁴, William³, William², William¹.)

(64.) Sarah Bradshaw⁵—a daughter of Elizabeth Carver and David Bradshaw—was born in Buckingham, 1780, 9th month 29; married Joseph Taylor. His will is dated 1842, 8th month 10, and recorded in Will Book No. 13, December 7, 1848. He left a widow and children:

260. Banner Taylor.
261. Watson W. Taylor.
262. Seraphina Taylor.
263. Mary Taylor.

(Elizabeth⁴, William³, William², William¹.)

(65.) William Bradshaw⁵—a son of Elizabeth Carver and David Bradshaw—was born in Buckingham, 1782, 6th month 8; married Martha Coombs. He died leaving children:

264. Phebe Bradshaw. } Know nothing.
265. Isaac Bradshaw. }

(Elizabeth[4], William[3], William[2], William[1].)

(66.) Sidney Bradshaw[5]—another daughter of Elizabeth Carver and David Bradshaw, her husband—was born 1784, 4th month 10; married Jonathan Paist in 1805. He died in February, 1870. His will is dated 1867, 9th month 21, and recorded in Will Book No. 17, page 369, February 24, 1870. Sidney died 1861, 3d month 13. She had children:

266. Minerva S. Paist, b. 1806.
267. David Bradshaw Paist, b. 1808.
268. J. Monroe Paist, b. 1819.
269. Eliza A. Paist, b. 1810.

(Elizabeth[4], William[3], William[2], William[1].)

(67.) David Bradshaw, Jr.[5]—a son of Elizabeth Carver and David Bradshaw,—was born 1786, 4th month 21; married 1824, 2d month 25, Malicent Large, daughter of Joseph, and died intestant, 1854, 11th month 18. His children are:

270. David Heston Bradshaw.
271. Joseph Bradshaw.
272. Lewis W. Bradshaw.
273. Seraphina T. Bradshaw.
274. Rebecca Bradshaw.
275. Anna M. Bradshaw.
276. Mary Elizabeth Bradshaw.

(68.) Ruth Bradshaw—another daughter of Elizabeth Carver and David Bradshaw, her husband—was born in Buckingham, 1789, 9th month 12; married Moses Meredith, son of Hugh. Had children:

277. Ruth Ann Meredith.
278. Anna Maria Meredith.
279. Watson Meredith, d. young.

(Elizabeth[4], William[3], William[2], William[1].)

(69.) James Bradshaw[5]—another son of Elizabeth Carver and David Bradshaw, her husband—was born in Buckingham, 1791, 6th month 15. Know nothing of him.

(Elizabeth[4], William[3], William[2], William[1].)

(70.) Elizabeth Bradshaw[5]—another daughter of Elizabeth Carver and David Bradshaw—was born in Buckingham 1799, 6th month 25; married Sylvester Linburg of Buckingham. Had children.

280. John Roland Linburg.
281. Howard Linburg.
282. Benjamin Morris Linburg.
283. Ruth Ann Linburg.

(Mary⁴, William³, William², William¹.)

(71.) William Kirk⁵—son of Mary Carver and John Kirk—was born in Buckingham, 1787, 11th month 15, and was twice married: first, to Phebe Malone, by whom he had his children; secondly, to Mary Hutchinson. He died in June, 1869. His will was proven July 1, 1869, in Will Book No. 17, page 274. His son, John M. Kirk, and Benjamin S. Rich were his executors. His children are:

284. Rebecca Kirk, b. 1812, 1 mo. 20.
285. Spencer W. Kirk.
286. Stephen Smith Kirk.
287. John M. Kirk.
288. W. Mitchel Kirk.
289. Albert Kirk.
290. Nelson Kirk.
291. Charles Kirk, unm.
292 Mary Ellen Kirk, d. young.

(Mary⁴, William³, William², William¹.)

(72.) Sarah Kirk⁵—a daughter of Mary Carver and John Kirk, her husband—was born in Buckingham, 1790, 12th month 2; married Benjamin Doan of Upper Makefield, who died intestate in 1865, leaving no widow, but the following children:

293. Evelina Doan.
294. John K. Doan.
295. Eleazer Doan.
296. Amos Doan.
297. William K. Doan.
298. Benjamin C. Doan.
299. Stephen K. Doan.
300. Theodore J. Doan.
301. Mary Doan.
302. Sarah S. Doan.
303. Miranda K. Doan.

(Mary[4], William[3], William[2], William[1].)

(73.) Mary Kirk[5]—another daughter of Mary Carver and John Kirk, her husband—was born in Buckingham, 1792, 5th month 5; married John Betts, Jr., in 1812, 1st month 23, who died intestate about October 1, 1865. His son, Simpson Carey Betts, administered to his estate. Had children:

304. Randolph K. Betts, b. 1813, 1 mo. 27, d. 1814, 1 mo. 3.
305. Mary Kirk Betts, b. 1815, 5 mo. 19, d. 1820, 11 mo. 20.
306. Sarah Ann Betts, b. 1816, 10 mo. 14.
307. Letitia Anderson Betts, b. 1821, 11 mo. 8.
308. Simpson Carey Betts, b. 1825, 6 mo. 23.
308½. Martha M. Betts, b. 1827, 6 mo. 19, d. 1832, 7 mo. 2.

Mary Kirk, the mother, died 1879, 1st month 29.

(Mary[4], William[3], William[2], William.[1])

(74.) John Kirk[5]—another son of Mary Carver and John Kirk, her husband—was born in Buckingham, 1795, 8th month 26; married Rachel Kirk, daughter of Joseph, and died intestate in 1835, leaving a widow and children:

309. John Wilson Kirk.
310. Joseph Comley Kirk.
311. Thomas Harvey Kirk.
312. Stephen L. Kirk.

The first two were above the age of fourteen, and presented their petition to the Orphans' Court at December Term, 1837, for guardians. At the same court, Rachel, the mother, presented a petition for guardians for Thomas Harvey Kirk and Stephen L. Kirk, being under fourteen years old. Isaac C. Kirk administered to the estate.

(Mary[4], William[3], William[2], William[1].)

(75.) Isaac C. Kirk[5]—another son of Mary Carver and John Kirk, her husband—was born 1797, 11th month 6; married, 1820, 10th month 12, to Eliza Coates, and died 1878, 9th month 29. His will is dated 1878, 3d month 5, and recorded in Will Book No. 20, page 239. Emmor Walton, a son-in-law, was the executor. The children are:

313. Watson W. Kirk, b. 1829, 9 mo. 15.
314. Maria L. Kirk, b. 1826, 1 mo. 4.
315. Mary Jane Kirk, b. 1827, 12 mo. 2.
316. Rachel Kirk, b. 1830.
317. Anna L. Kirk, b. 1835, 6 mo. 22.

WILLIAM CARVER

(Mary[4], William[3], William[2], William.[1])

(76.) Stephen Kirk[5]—another son of Mary Carver and John Kirk, her husband—was born 1800, 1st month 8; married Anna Large, and died in Buckingham about September 1, 1878. His will is dated 1877, 5th month 24, recorded in Will Book, No. 20, page 233. He left a widow, but no children.

(Joseph[4], Joseph[3], William[2], William[1].)

(77.) Cornelius Carver[5]—a son of Joseph Carver and Mary Van Sant, his wife—was born in Buckingham; married Mary Martendale, and died in February, 1818, before his father made his will. His will bears date, 1818, 1st month 27, and proven in Will Book No. 9, page 242. He left a widow and children:

318. Rebecca V. Carver, } Each under the age of twenty-one when their
319. Sarah Ann Carver, } father died.

(Joseph[4], Joseph[3], William[2], William[1].)

(78.) Garret V. Carver[5], of Northampton Twp—another son of Joseph Carver and Mary Van Sant, his wife—married Elizabeth Kruisen, and died in March, 1858. His will was proven March 25, 1858, in Will Book No. 14, page 274. His wife Elizabeth, his son Joseph V., and his son-in-law Jacob V. Cornell were his executors. His children are:

320. Derrick K. Carver, b. 1815, 1 mo. 23.
321. Joseph V. Carver, b. 1816, 5 mo. 15.
322. Mary Carver.

There were two other girls who died at the age of nineteen.

(Joseph[4], Joseph[3], William[2], William[1].)

(80.) Mary V. Carver[5]—a daughter of Joseph Carver and Mary Van Sant, his wife—was born 1785, 7th month 7; married Thomas Bye, Jr., of Buckingham, 1807, 4th month 22. She died 1836, 8th month 15. Had children:

323. Thomas W. Bye, b. 1807, 12 mo. 20.
324. Joseph C. Bye, b. 1810, 6 mo. 6.
325. Allen R. Bye, b. 1813, 9 mo. 6.

(Joseph[4], Joseph[3], William[2], William[1].)

(81.) Martha Carver[5]—another daughter of Joseph Carver and Mary Van Sant, his wife—married John Fretz. They had no children. She died in the Boro of Doylestown, 1856, 12th month 13, and he in 1872, 12th month 4.

(Joseph⁴, Joseph³, William², William¹.)

(82.) Joel Carver⁵—another son of Joseph Carver and Mary Van Sant, his wife—was born in Solesbury, 1798, 3d month 5. He was twice married. His first wife was Lydia Gill, by whom he had one child. Lydia died and he married Hannah McDowell, daughter of William and Esther Carver, his wife. They had one child. Joel died in Lambertville, N. J., 1881, 9th month 2, æt. 81 years, 5 months, 28 days. His children are:

326. Anna G. Carver.
327. Angeline Carver, b. 1842, 6 mo. 9, d. 1842, 7 mo. 6.

(Joel⁴, Joseph³, William², William¹.)

(83.) Joseph Carver⁵—a son of Joel Carver and Ann Smith, his wife—was born in 1777; married Ann Carey, and lived in Northampton, Bucks Co., Pa. He died intestate, leaving one child:

328. Jane Carver, b. 1798, 11 mo. 12.

(Joel⁴, Joseph³, William², William¹.)

(84.) Robert Carver⁵—another son of Joel Carver and Ann Smith, his wife—married Mary Smith, 1807, 10th month 18, and resided in Northampton Twp, Bucks Co., Pa. He died there 1851, 12th month, intestate. Mary, his wife, died 1866, 9th month 30. Had children:

329. Joseph Carver.
330. Smith Carver.
331. Elizabeth Carver.
332. Joel Carver.
333. Samuel Carver, d. unm.
334. William Carver.
335. Ann Carver.
336. Mary Carver.
337. John Carver.
338. Hannah Carver, unm.
339. Jane Carver, unm.

(Joel⁴, Joseph³, William², William¹.)

(85.) Ann Carver⁵—a daughter of Joel Carver and Ann Smith, his wife—of Northampton Twp, was born 1786, 4th month 14, and married four times: first, to Abraham Lloyd; second, to Richard Leedom; third, to Enos Morris of Newtown; fourth, to George Stuckert. She died in the Boro of Doylestown, Pa., 1852, 9th month 21. Her will bears date 1851, 5th month 20, and proven in Will Book No. 13, page 566, October 4, 1852. She had but one child and that was by Abraham Lloyd, to wit:

340. John Lloyd, b. 1809, 2 mo. 16.

WILLIAM CARVER

(Joel[4], Joseph[3], William[2], William[1].)

(86.) Joel Carver[5] of Northampton—another son of Joel Carver and Ann Smith, his wife—married Maria Vanarsdale and died leaving children:

341. Alfred Carver.
342. Euphemia V. Carver.
343. Garret Carver.

(Joel[4], Joseph[3], William[2], William[1].)

(89.) Hanna Carver[5]—a daughter of Joel Carver and Ann Smith, his wife—was twice married: first, to George Hobensack of Northampton; and second, to George Willard, who kept the Lady Washington Hotel, on what was called the middle road to Philadelphia. Her children were by her first husband, to wit:

344. Joel Hobensack.
345. John Hobensack.
346. George Hobensack.
347. Ann Hobensack.

(John[4], Joseph[3], William[2], William[1].)

(90.) Joseph Carver[5]—a son of John Carver and Ann Carver, his wife—married Hannah Lovett, and died in Buckingham in February, 1851. His will is dated March 10, 1850, and proven February 15, 1851, in Will Book No. 13, page 36. His children are:

348. John J. Carver.
349. Samuel L. Carver.
350. James Carver.
351. Joseph Carver.
352. William Carver.
353. Clemens Carver, d. young.
354. Hannah Carver.
355. Audery Carver.
356. Mary Ann Carver.

(John[4], Joseph[3], William[2], William[1].)

(91.) Isaac Carver[5]—another son of John Carver and Ann Carver, his wife—of Buckingham, married Sarah Martendale, and died, 1855, 6th month 7, leaving but one child:

357. George W. Carver, b. 1810, 10 mo. 11.

(John⁴, Joseph³, William², William¹.)

(92.) Eli Carver⁵—another son of John Carver and Ann Carver, his wife—was constable of Buckingham Twp; married Mary Dunlap, and died leaving children:

358. Mary Ann Carver, d. unm.
359. John Carver, d. childless.
360. Charles F. Carver, d. childless.
361. Joseph Carver, d. childless.
362. James Carver, d. childless.
363. Elizabeth A. Carver, b. 1812, 8 mo. 25.
364. Maria Carver, d. childless.

(John⁴, Joseph³, William², William¹.)

(93.) John Carver⁵—another son of John Carver and Ann Carver, his wife—married Mary Martendale, who was born about 1791, 5th month. He died in Buckingham in April, 1853. His will is dated July 8, 1852, and proven May 5, 1853, in Will Book No. 13, page 568. His widow died in Buckingham, 1881, 11th month 10, æt. 90 years, 6 months. His children are:

365. John Carver.
366. Amos M. Carver, b. 1813, 10 mo. 24.
367. Jesse M. Carver, b. 1816.
368. Adin Carver, b. 1830.
369. Yardley Carver.
370. Oliver Carver.
371. Wilson Carver.
372. Maria Carver.
373. Keziah Carver.
374. Caroline Carver.
375. Mary Carver.
376. Cynthia Carver.
377. Margery Ann Carver.
378. Rebecca Carver.

(John⁴, Joseph³, William², William¹.)

(95.) Miller D. Carver⁵—a son of John and Ann Carver, his wife—married Ann Hanen and died in Ohio in 1833.

(John⁴, Joseph³, William², William¹.)

(97.) Miles Carver⁵—a son of John and Ann Carver, his wife—married and died leaving four or five children. The eldest was:

379. Ely Carver.

(John⁴, Joseph³, William², William¹.)

(98.) Martha Carver⁵—a daughter of John and Ann Carver, his wife—was born in Buckingham, and twice married: first, to Jesse Erving of Chester Co., Pa., and secondly, to John Walton of Chester Co. She died. Her children are:

380. Nellie Erving.
381. Harriet Walton.
382. John Walton.
383. Amy Walton.

(John⁴, Joseph³, William², William¹.)

(99.) Phebe Carver⁵—a daughter of John Carver and Ann Carver, his wife—was born in Buckingham, Saturday, 1787, 11th month 10; married Samuel Gilbert and died in Philadelphia, Monday, 1862, 3d month 10. She was buried at Attleborough, now Langhorn, in the Baptist burying ground. The following are her children, ten in number:

384. Mahlon Gilbert, b. 1810, 5 mo., Thursday.
385. George W. Gilbert, b. 1812, 8 mo. 25, Tuesday.
386. Lydia Ann Gilbert, b. 1814, 11 mo. 28, Monday.
387. Jonathan Gilbert, b. 1816, 11 mo. 10, Sunday.
388. David Gilbert, b. 1819, 10 mo. 15, Friday.
389. John Gilbert, b. 1821, 11 mo. 8, Thursday.
390. Rebecca Gilbert, b. 1824, 1 mo. 7, Thursday.
391. Howard Gilbert, b. 1826, 7 mo. 26, Wednesday.
392. Asa Comley Gilbert, b. 1828, 10 mo. 17, Friday, } Twins.
393. Agnes C. Gilbert, b. 1828, 10 mo. 17, Friday, }

(John⁴, Joseph³, William², William¹.)

(100.) Mary Carver⁵—another daughter of John Carver and Ann Carver, his wife—was born in Buckingham; married Reuben Haines, and died leaving children:

394. Joseph Haines.
395. Annie Haines.
396. Margaret Haines.

(John⁴, Joseph³, William², William¹.)

(101.) Amy Carver⁵—another daughter of John Carver and Ann Carver, his wife—was born 1790, 7th month 30; married Amos Addis of Northampton in 1811. He died in January, 1859. His will was proven, February 1, 1859, in Will Book No. 14, page 407. She died, 1867, 4th month. Her children are:

397. John Carver Addis, b. 1815, 8 mo. 10.
398. Ellen Addis, b. 1812, 11 mo.
399. Isaac Clarkson Addis, b. 1819, 9 mo. 30.
400. Eliza Ann Addis, b. 1824, 9 mo.
401. Mary Hutchinson Addis, b. 1830, 10 mo.

(John[4], Joseph[3], William[2], William[1].)

(102.) Ann Carver[5]—another daughter of John Carver and Ann, his wife—was born in Buckingham, 1795, 3d month 10, and was twice married: first, to John Short of Cecil Co., Maryland—they had three children; secondly, to Samuel Houpt of Kennet Square, Chester Co., Pa.—they had two children; to wit:

401 ½. Isabella Short.
402. William Short.
403. John Short.
404. Robert L. Houpt, b. 1829, 10 mo. 1.
405. Ann Eliza Houpt, b. 1832, 5 mo. 9.

(Ruth[4], Joseph[3], William[2], William[1].)

(103.) Joseph C. Terry[5]—a son of Ruth Carver and John Terry, Esq., her husband—was born in 1792; married Mary Vansant of Yardleyville, and died in Doylestown, Pa. Had children:

406. Harvey Terry, b. February, 1821.
407. Isaiah B. Terry, b. 1823.
408. Eliza Jane Terry, b. 1827, 3 mo. 6.
409. Hanna A. Terry, b. 1829, 5 mo. 8.
410. John V. Terry, b. 1831, 8 mo.
411. Mary Ann Terry, b. 1834, 10 mo.
412. Oliver T. Terry, b. 1837.
413. Caroline Terry, b. 1825, d. young.

(Ruth[4], Joseph[3], William[2], William[1].)

(104.) Martha Terry[5]—a daughter of Ruth Carver and John Terry, Esq., her husband—was born in 1795, 6th month 27, and married John Beans, Esq., of Hatborough, 1818, 11th month 19. She died 1871, 2d month 23. Had children:

414. Mary Ann Beans, b. 1819, 11 mo. 22.
415. Sarah T. Beans, b. 1821, 11 mo. 3.
416. Amanda Beans, b. 1823, 11 mo. 9.
417. Eliza L. Beans, b. 1826, 9 mo. 26.

(Ruth[4], Joseph[4], William[2], William[1].)

(105.) James Terry[5]—another son of Ruth Carver and John Terry, Esq., her husband—was born in Wrightstown, Bucks Co., Pa., 1797, 10th month 2. He was married three times: first, to Aletha Baily; second, to Amanda Reed; third, to M. Williams. He resided in Philadelphia. Had eleven children by his first wife, four by his second, but none by his third, as follows:

418. Joshua Vansant Terry, b. 1822, 1 mo. 11.
419. Martha Terry, b. 1825, 11 mo. 10.
420. William Terry, b. 1828, 9 mo. 12, } Twins.
421. Samuel B. Terry, b. 1828, 9 mo. 12, }
422. James M. Terry, b. 1831, 3 mo. 19, at 5 years.
423. Aletha W. Terry, b. 1833, 4 mo. 21.
424. Edward Terry, b. 1835, 6 mo. 19.
425. Wesley B. Terry, b. 1838, 1 mo. 26.
426. Mary V. Terry, b. 1839, 8 mo. 3.
427. Rachel Ann Terry, b. 1841, 8 mo. 11.
428. Ruth Terry, b. 1844, 1 mo. 20.
429. Sarah A. Terry, b. 1848, 12 mo. 28, by second wife.
430. Margaret Emma Terry, b. 1851, 2 mo. 5, by second wife.
431. Isaac Kline Terry, b. 1854, 4 mo. 5, by second wife.
432. Joseph Carver Terry, b. 1856, 6 mo. 1, by second wife.

(Martha[4], Joseph[3], William[2], William[1].)

(105½.) John Price, Esq.[5]—a son of Martha Carver and Smith Price, her husband—married Elizabeth Kirk and died in November, 1828. Their children are:

433. Charles M. Price.
434. Kirk J. Price.
435. Stephen K. Price.
436. Sarah Price.
437. Smith Price.
438. Preston Price.
439. Hannah Price.
440. John Price.

(William[4], Joseph[3], William[2], William[1].)

(106.) Ann Carver[5]—a daughter of William Carver and Martha Addis, his wife—was born 1777, 1st month 22, died 1778, 8th month 24.

(William[4], Joseph[3], William[2], William[1].)

(107.) Martha Carver[5]—another daughter of William Carver and Martha Addis, his wife—was born 1778, 11th month 15; married William Pool, of Solebury, 1801, 1st month 15, at Neshaminy Church. William was born 1776, 2d month 18. Martha died 1854, 12th month 10. Their children are:

441. William C. Pool, b. 1801, 11 mo. 13.
442. Izri Pool, b. 1803, 9 mo. 29.
443. Edward Q. Pool, b. 1809, 5 mo. 1.
444. Thomas Pool, b. 1811, 2 mo. 5.
445. Martha Pool, b. 1815, 12 mo. 18.

(William⁴, Joseph³, William², William¹.)

(108.) John Carver⁵—a son of William Carver and Martha Addis, his wife—was born 1780, 10th month 15. He enlisted in the war of 1812, and was killed at the battle of Lundy's Lane. Not married.

(William⁴, Joseph³, William², William¹.)

(109.) Elizabeth Carver⁵—another daughter of William Carver and Martha Addis, his wife—was born in Solebury, 1783, 4th month 10; married William Streeper of Solebury, who died intestate, 1827, 1st month 13. Elizabeth afterwards married Jesse Edwards of Northampton Twp. He died intestate in March, 1849, and she the latter part of December, 1855. Her will is dated June 21, 1852, and recorded in Will Book No. 14, page 46, 1856, 4th month 4. Her children were by her first husband, as follows:

446. Catharine Streeper, d. unm.
447. Margaret Streeper, d. unm.
448. Martha A. Streeper.
449. Elizabeth Streeper.

The two last were in their minority when their father died. Margaret and Catharine died unmarried; Margaret before her mother.

(William⁴, Joseph³, William², William¹.)

(110.) Joseph Carver⁵—another son of William Carver and Martha Addis, his wife—was born in Solebury, 1785, 9th month 10; enlisted in the war of 1812, and was wounded in the battle at Lundy's Lane. After the war he returned home and was known as "Fifing Joe," being a superior player on the instrument. He never married.

(William⁴, Joseph³, William², William¹.)

(111.) Hannah Carver⁵—another daughter of William Carver and Martha Addis, his wife—was born, 1787, 9th month 10, in Solebury; married John Kimble of Buckingham, and died in March, 1863. Had children:

450. John Kimble, Jr., b. in 1816.
451. Martha Kimble, b. in 1812.
452. Hannah Kimble, b. in 1814.
453. Elizabeth Kimble, b. in 1819.
454. George Washington Kimble, b. in 1822.
455. Henry H. Kimble, b. in 1824.

(William⁴, Joseph³, William², William¹.)

(113.) Izri Carver⁵—another son of William Carver and Martha Addis, his wife—was born in Solebury, 1792, 9th month 6, and married Mary Hartley. His children are:

456. William Carver.
457. Martha R. Carver.
458. Elizabeth H. Carver.

WILLIAM CARVER

(Elizabeth[4], Henry[3], William[2], William[1].)

(114.) Giles Oldden[5]—a son of Elizabeth Carver and Aaron Oldden, her husband. Know nothing more.

(Elizabeth[4], Henry[3], William[2], William[1].)

(115.) Catharine Oldden[5]—a daughter of Elizabeth Carver and Aaron Oldden—married Smith Kepler of Plumstead. They had no children.

(Elizabeth[4], Henry[3], William[2], William[1].)

(116.) Rachel Oldden[5]—another daughter of Elizabeth Carver and Aaron Oldden—married Thomas Elton, 1817, 9th month 13, and died 1851, 8th month 15, æt. 59 years. Their children are:

459. Rebecca Gillingham Elton, b. 1818, 6 mo. 25, d. 1818, 9 mo. 21.
460. Elizabeth Catharine Elton, b. 1820, 3 mo. 2.
461. Josephine Gillingham Elton, b. 1827, 3 mo. 27, d. 1850, 3 mo, 13.

(Rachel[4], Henry[3], William[2], William[1].)

(117.) Hugh B. Ely—a son of Rachel Carver and Jesse Ely, her husband—was born in Buckingham in 1792, 11th month 3; married Sarah Oldden of New Jersey, and died intestate, 1850, 8th month. Had children:

462. Achsah M. Ely, b. 1815, 9 mo. 25.
463. Mary Anna Ely, b. 1816, 11 mo. 20.
464. Francenia Ely, b. 1818, 1 mo. 26.
465. Joseph Oldden Ely, b. 1820, 2 mo. 10.
466. Alfred Ely, b. 1822, 9 mo. 25, d. young.
467. Charles Bennington Ely, b. 1824, 9 mo. 1.
468. William Penn Ely, b. 1827, 2 mo. 6.

(118.) Charles Ely—another son of Rachel Carver and Jesse Ely, her husband—was born in Solebury, 1794, and died unmarried.

(120.) William C. Ely—another son of Rachel Carver and Jesse Ely, her husband—was born in Solebury, 1801, 3d month 17. He married Lydia D. Hulse, who was born 1817, 12th month 1. He died 1857, 11th month 27. Had children:

469. Catharine O. Ely, b. 1836, 5 mo. 5, d. 1853, 4 mo. 30.
470. Hugh B. Ely, b. 1838, 3 mo. 9.
471. Rachel S. Ely, b. 1840, 6 mo. 29.
472. Elizabeth C. Ely, b. 1842, 10 mo. 13.
473. Holmes D. Ely, b. 1845, 3 mo. 11.
474. Richard Watson Ely, b. 1847, 3 mo. 6, d. 1848, 1 mo. 16.
475. Sarah Y. Ely, b. 1849, 4 mo. 22.
476. Thomas H. Ely, b. 1851, 10 mo. 16, d. 1855, 7 mo. 13.
477. William C. Ely, Jr., b. 1854, 9 mo. 30, d. 1875, 4 mo. 7.

(Rachel[4], Henry[3], William[2], William[1].)

(122.) Henry C. Ely—another son of Rachel Carver and Jesse Ely, her husband—was born in Solebury, 1811, 10th month 8; went South, and probably died there unmarried.

(Thomas[4], Henry[3], William[2], William[1].)

(125.) Samuel Carver, M.D.[5]—a son of Thomas Carver and Sarah Harrold, his wife. He studied medicine and practiced a short time in Bucks Co., Pa. He was a splendid-looking man; started to go to China, and the last place he was heard from was Calcutta, Hindoostan.

(Thomas[4], Henry[3], William[2], William[1].)

(126.) David Carver[5]—another son of Thomas Carver and Sarah Harrold, his wife—married Ann Walker, a daughter of Robert of Buckingham, 1815, 1st month 11. They had several children, but only three lived to grow up; the others died in infancy. His wife, Ann, died in Solebury. He afterwards married, a second time, the widow of Dr. Henrie of New York. Her maiden name was Abby Cattell. Had no children by her. He died in Philadelphia, leaving children:

478. Elizabeth W. Carver, b. 1817, 9 mo. 26.
479. Asenath Carver, b. 1819, 12 mo. 19.
480. Sarah Ann Carver, b. 1829, 10 mo. 25.

(Thomas[4], Henry[3], William[2], William[1].)

(127.) Henry Carver—another son of Thomas Carver and Sarah Harrold, his wife—went West when a young man.

(Thomas[4], Henry[3], William[2], William[1].)

(128.) Elizabeth H. Carver[5]—a daughter of Thomas Carver and Sarah Harrold, his wife—married Dr. Jesse Beans, a son of Joseph, and grandson of Jacob Beans who married Sarah Hartley, 1815, 12th month 13. No children.

(129.) James Carver—another son of Thomas Carver and Sarah Harrold, his wife—went West with his brother Henry. Know nothing of either.

(130.) Rachel Carver—a daughter of John Carver and Sarah Ellicott, who was a daughter of Thomas of Carversville—was born 1785, 12th month 25; married Kimble Skelton of Solebury in 1844, 12th month 7. No children.

(131.) Thomas Carver—a son of John Carver and Sarah Ellicott—was born 1787, 4th month 23, and died at Carversville, Solebury Twp, Pa., where he kept store, 1853, 7th month 4. Unmarried.

WILLIAM CARVER

(John[4], Henry[3], William[2], William[1].)

(132.) Pamelia Carver[5]—another daughter of John Carver and Sarah Ellicott, his wife—was born 1792, 3d month 22; married Nicholas Wanamaker in 1811, and died in Solebury, 1858. She had eight children, to wit:

481. Anna Eliza Wanamaker, b. 1812, 8 mo. 16.
482. Letitia Wanamaker, b. 1817, 2 mo. 23.
483. Mary G. Wanamaker, b. 1819, 3 mo. 5.
484. Thomas C. Wanamaker, b. 1824, 8 mo. 10.
485. John E. Wanamaker, b. 1826, 7 mo. 6.
486. Anna U. Wanamaker, b. 1830, 1 mo. 4.
487. Alfred Wanamaker, b. 1832, 1 mo. 11.
488. Henry C. Wanamaker, b. 1834, 12 mo. 15.

(133.) Ann Carver—another daughter of John and Sarah—was born 1794, 11th month 21, and died unmarried.

(John[4], Henry[3], William[2], William[1].)

(134.) Sarah Ann Carver[5]—another daughter of John Carver and Sarah Ellicott, his wife—was born 1799, 3d month 2; married Joseph Prior Shaw in 1828, and died in 1847. Their children are:

489. Alfred Shaw, b. 1830.
490. Anna Shaw, b. 1831, d. 1837.
491. Marietta Shaw, b. 1834.
492. John Wilson Shaw, b. 1837.

(John[4], Henry[3], William[2], William[1].)

(135.) Letitia Ellicott Carver[5]—another daughter of John Carver and Sarah Ellicott, his wife—was born 1802, 12th month 9; married Alexander Johnson Case, 1824, 12th month 28, and died 1856, 1st month 9. Had children:

493. J. Watson Case, b. 1826, 11 mo. 24.
494. Sarah A. Case, b. 1828, 8 mo. 30.
495. Willlam E. Case, b. 1831, 1 mo. 2.
496. Caroline B. Case, b. 1833, 2 mo. 14.
497. Henry C. Case, b. 1835, 8 mo. 9.
498. Rebecca C. Case, b. 1839, 10 mo. 9.
499. Elizabeth H. Case, b. 1836, 12 mo. 13, d. 1838, 10 mo. 16.
500. Samuel C. Case, b. 1843, 8 mo. 2.

(John[4], Henry[3], William[2], William[1].)

(136.) John Ellicott Carver[5]—another son of John Carver and Sarah Ellicott, his wife—was born 1805, 11th month 7; married Eliza E. Nicholson, a widow, whose maiden name was Crim, in 1836. He resided in Philadelphia, and was an architect of merit. He died there in April, 1859; his widow in 1869. His children are:

501. Thomas J. Carver, b. 1838.
502. William Henry Harrison Carver, b. 1841, 3 mo. 18.

(John[4], Henry[3], William[2], William[1].)

(137.) Rebecca Gillingham Carver[5]—daughter of John Carver and Sarah Ellicott—was born 1809, 8th month 6; married Samuel Carr of Plumstead, 1839, 2d month 21, and died 1842, 6th month 1. She had one child:

503. Ann Rebecca Carr, b. 1842, 4 mo. 12, d. 1864, 6 mo. 13, unm.

(John[4], Henry[3], William[2], William[1].)

(138.) Henry Ellicott Carver[5]—another son of John Carver and Sarah Ellicott—was born 1815, 3d month 13; married Elizabeth Shaw, daughter of John of Plumstead, and died near Carversville, 1877, 2d month 22. He had one child:

504. Sarah Grace Carver, d. 1857, 10 mo. 30, unm.

(139.) Thomas Carver—a son of Joseph Carver and Hannah Carey, his wife—was born in Plumstead Twp, 1778, 9th month 9. When a young man he went to Harrisville, Harrison Co., Ohio. There he married Tamson Gray, and resided there till his death, which took place 1855, 10 mo. 13. His children are:

505. Joseph Carver, b. 1818, 11 mo. 7, d. 1845, 5 mo. 5.
506. Elizabeth Ann Carver, b. 1821, 4 mo. 29.
507. Hannah Carver, b. 1824, 4 mo. 6, d. 1833, 7 mo. 5.
508. Julia Ann Carver, b. 1830, 11 mo. 14.
509. Mary J. Carver, b. 1827, 7 mo. 2.
510. Emily Carver, b. 1835, 5 mo. 15.

(Joseph[4], Henry[3], William[2], William[1].)

(140.) Henry Carver[5]—another son of Joseph Carver and Hannah Carey, his wife—was born in Plumstead, 1790, 2d month 8, and married Hannah Paxson, daughter of Abraham, of Solebury 1815, 2d month 10. They lived in Carversville till the spring of 1825, when he moved to a farm which he had purchased, situate in the upper part of Buckingham Twp; the road called the Long Lane on the northwest and the street road separating the townships of Solebury and Buckingham. He sold this

WILLIAM CARVER

farm and in the spring of 1855 moved to a lot he purchased in Centreville, in Buckingham Twp. His wife died there, 1857, 2d month 11, in the evening. He then sold this lot and in the spring of 1857 moved to his son-in-law's, Joseph C. Slack, in Northampton Twp, Bucks Co., Pa. He died there 1863, 1st month 23, about half-past 12 o'clock noon, æt. 72 years, 11 months, 15 days. He had two children :

511. Elizabeth B. Carver, b. 1816, 2 mo. 17, d. 1887, 5 mo. 18.
512. Elias Carver, b. 1817, 10 mo. 2.

(Joseph[4], Henry[3], William[2], William[1].)

(141.) Rachel Carver[5]—a daughter of Joseph Carver and Hannah Carey, his wife—was born in Plumstead Twp, Bucks Co., Pa., 1794, 8th month 24. She married at Harrisville, Ohio, May 1816, Joseph Broadhurst, son of Thomas. Joseph died at Greenville, Buckingham Twp, Pa., 1868, 3d month 13. Had children :

513. Son born 1817, 3 mo. 26, and died same day.
514. Mary Anna Broadhurst, b. 1818, 9 mo. 6.
515. Samuel E. Broadhurst, 1823, 2 mo. 25.
516. Caroline L. Broadhurst, b. 1826, 10 mo. 17.

(Joseph[4], Henry[3], William[2], William[1].)

(142.) Mary Carver[5]—another daughter of Joseph Carver and Hannah Carey, his wife—was born in Plumstead Twp, 1789, 2d month 26; married Samuel Eastburn of Solebury, 1824, 4th month 14, and died in Buckingham of apoplexy, 1850, 4th month 6, æt. 52 years, 1 month, 8 days. Samuel married a second wife, a widow whose maiden name was Rachel Parry. His children were by his first wife :

517. Charles Eastburn, b. 1825, 5 mo. 24.
518. Henry C. Eastburn, b. 1827, 2 mo. 17.
519. Joseph C. Eastburn, b. 1829, 2 mo. 3, d. 1830, 3 mo. 5.
520. Edward Eastburn, b. 1831, 1 mo. 9.
521. Hannah C. Eastburn, b. 1833, 6 mo. 13.
522. Rachel Eastburn, b. 1835, 9 mo. 13, d. 1836, 9 mo. 13.

(Joseph[4], Henry[3], William[2], William[1].)

(143.) Anne Carver[5]—another daughter of Joseph Carver and Hannah Carey, his wife—was born at Carversville, Solebury Twp, Pa., 1802, 10th month 12; married Samuel Smith, son of George, 1836, 10th month 12. They bought a farm in Buckingham, on the Durham Road above Centreville, and moved there, where she died, 1883, 6th month 13. Samuel died 1884. Had one child :

523. Rachel Smith, b. 1837, 12 mo. 8, d. 1901, 12 mo. 29, unm.

(Joseph⁴, Henry³, William², William¹.)

(144.) Eli Carver⁵—another son of Joseph Carver and Hannah Carey, his wife—was born at Carversville, Bucks Co., Pa., 1804, 5th month 4. He married, 1832, 11th month, Martha P. Ross, daughter of Cephas of Plumstead. Cephas was a brother of Judge John Ross of Doylestown, and afterward a Justice of the Supreme Court of Pennsylvania. Eli died at Buckingham in the fall of 1871, leaving a widow and children :

524. Mary Anna B. Carver, b. 1833, 8 mo. 2.
525. Jenkens R. Carver, b. 1835, } Twins.
526. Joseph C. Carver, b. 1835, }
527. Elizabeth F. Carver, b. 1837, 7 mo. 7.
528. Hannah C. Carver, b. 1838, 10 mo.
529. Charles R. Carver, d. at about 10 years.
530. Cephas R. Carver.
531. Cecilia E. Carver.
532. Eli C. Carver.
533. Martha Emma Carver.
534. Eber Leamon Carver.
535. Walter Scott Carver, b. 1857, 2 mo. 6.
536. Edward Paxson Carver.

(Joseph⁴, Henry³, William², William¹.)

(145.) Julia H. Carver⁵—another daughter of Joseph Carver and Hannah Carey, his wife—was born in Carversville, Pa., 1809, 9th month 28; married Elihu W. Allen, 1830, 4th month 7, and died at Centre Hill, Solebury Twp, 1877, 7th month 14, æt. 67 years, 9 months, 16 days. Had children :

537. Oliver C. Allen, b. 1831, 1 mo. 3, d. 1836, 8 mo. 11, in Ohio.
538. Alfred E. Allen, b. 1832, 12 mo. 30.
539. Caroline W. Allen, b. 1834, 10 mo. 28.
540. Joseph C. Allen, b. 1837, 7 mo. 15.
541. Hannah A. Allen, b. 1841, 4 mo. 17, d. 1844.
542. Mary B. Allen, b. 1843, 5 mo. 18.
543. Martha C. Allen, b. 1845, 12 mo. 6.
544. Elizabeth C. Allen, b. 1848, 10 mo. 3, d. 1850.
545. Rachel S. Allen, b. 1852, 4 mo. 30.

(Benjamin⁴, Henry³, William², William¹.)

(146.) Amos Carver⁵—a son of Benjamin Carver and Sarah Kirk, his wife—was born in Plumstead Twp, 1791, 5th month 22; married Elizabeth Lewis, daughter of John. His children are :

WILLIAM CARVER

545½. Rachel Carver, b. 1814, 10 mo. 20.
546. Benjamin Carver, Jr.; went to Canada.
547. Mordecai Carver, b. 1818, 12 mo. 31.
548. Sarah Carver, b. 1820, 9 mo. 23.
549. Jane Carver, b. 1823, 10 mo. 19.
550. Samuel Carver, b. 1826, 3 mo.
551. Caroline Carver, b. 1828, 3 mo. 22.
552. Mary Carver; went to Canada.
553. Lewis Carver, b. 1832, 10 mo. 13.
554. Ruth Ann Carver, b. 1835, 2 mo. 8.

(Benjamin[4], Henry[3], William[2], William[1].)

(147.) William Carver[5]—another son of Benjamin Carver and Sarah Kirk, his wife—was born in Plumstead, 1793, 3d month 6; married; went to Berks Co. and married a German woman, and died there. His children as far as is known are:

555. William Carver.
556. Thomas Carver.
557. Levi Carver.
558. ———— Carver.

(Benjamin[4], Henry[3], William[2], William[1].)

(148.) Jesse Carver[5]—another son of Benjamin Carver and Sarah Kirk, his wife—was born in Plumstead, 1797, 3d month 24; married Euphemia Ely, daughter of Samuel and Grace Heverlin, 1824, 12th month 8, and died 1838, leaving four children, viz:

559. Alfred Carver, b. 1827, 10 mo. 12.
560. Samuel S. Carver, b. 1830, 12 mo. 20.
561. Cynthia A. Carver, b. 1833, 8 mo. 8.
562. Sophia Carver, b. 1837, 4 mo. 24.

(Benjamin[4], Henry[3], William[2], William[1].)

(149.) Cynthia Carver[5]—a daughter of Benjamin Carver and Sarah Kirk, his wife—was born in Plumstead, 1800, 8th month 19; married Isaac Black, 1817, and died 1869, 1st month 10. Had children:

563. Sophia Black, b. 1818, 4 mo. 12.
564. Sarah Ann Black, b. 1820, 11 mo. 20, d. 1823, 12 mo. 16.
565. William Black, b. 1823, 1 mo. 5.
566. Catharine Black, b. 1825, 2 mo. 6, d. 1845, 2 mo. 29, unm.
567. Ann Elizabeth Black, b. 1827, 10 mo. 13.
568. Levi Black, b. 1829, 12 mo. 28.
569. Isaac C. Black, b. 1831, 9 mo. 26.
570. Ezra W. Black, b. 1833, 12 mo. 16.
571. Abraham Black, b. 1836, 5 mo. 12.
572. Jesse L. Black, b. 1838, 8 mo. 23.

(Benjamin[4], Henry[3], William[2], William[1].)

(150.) Rachel Carver[5]—another daughter of Benjamin Carver and Sarah Kirk, his wife—was born in Plumstead, 1802, 12th month 3; married Anthony Fly, son of Frederick, 1823, 3d month 23, and died in Philadelphia, 1882, 1st month 15, in her 80th year. She had children:

573. Jane Eliza Coe Fly, b. 1824, 1 mo. 25.
574. Wilamina Maria Fly, b. 1826, 8 mo. 17, d. 1828, 1 mo. 25.
575. Levinia Fly, b. 1827, 3 mo. 7, d. 1827, 11 mo. 22.
576. Isaac Otis Fly, b. 1828, 12 mo. 21, died 1829, 4 mo. 16.
577. Sarah Ann Fly, b. 1830, 11 mo. 27, d. 1837, 1 mo. 18.
578. Martha B. Fly, b. 1833, 11 mo. 11.
579. Caroline Fly, b. 1836, 1 mo. 9, d. 1837, 1 mo. 20.
580. Mary H. Fly, b. 1837, 4 mo. 18.
581. Elizabeth Ann Fly, b. 1839, 11 mo. 26, d. 1874, 6 mo. 15.
582. Joseph Carver Fly, b. 1842, 1 mo. 1, unm.
583. Rachel Carrie Fly, b. 1847, 7 mo. 14, unm.

(Benjamin[4], Henry[3], William[2], William[1].)

(151.) Levi Carver[5]—another son of Benjamin Carver and Sarah Kirk, his wife—was born in Plumstead, 1805, 6th month 12; married Hannah Cosner, 1831, 4th month 6, and died in Northampton Twp, Bucks Co., 1881, 9th month 11, æt. 78 years. His children are:

584. Mary Ann Carver.
585. Lucinda Carver, b. 1828, 11 mo. 29, unm.
586. Elias Carver, b. 1832, 12 mo. 29.
587. Rebecca J. Carver, b. 1837, 3 mo. 19.
588. John W. Carver, b. 1839, 3 mo. 6.
589. Sarah E. Carver, b. 1841, 4 mo. 11, d. young.
590. Louisa Carver, b. 1843, 9 mo. 3.
591. Rachel Carver, b. 1845, 10 mo. 30.
592. Johanna Carver, b. 1847, 11 mo. 2.
593. Elmira Carver, b. 1848, 2 mo. 29.
594. William Carver, b. 1852, 3 mo. 28, d. young.

(Benjamin[4], Henry[3], William[2], William[1].)

(152.) Isaac Carver[5]—another son of Benjamin Carver and Sarah Kirk, his wife—was born in Plumstead, 1808, 1st month 6; married Elizabeth C. Biddle, 1835, 11th month 25, and resides in Philadelphia. His children are:

595. George W. Carver, b. 1836, 9 mo. 16.
596. Mary B. Carver, b. 1838, 11 mo. 5.
597. Charles C. Carver, b. 1841, 7 mo. 7, d. 1863, 1 mo. 25.
598. Sarah C. Carver, b. 1844, 1 mo. 27.

599. Emma T. Carver, 1846, 9 mo. 14, unm.
600. Anna E. Carver, b. 1849, 6 mo. 12, d. 1860, 6 mo. 4.
601. Henry C. Carver, b. 1852, 6 mo. 6, d. 1860, 11 mo. 20.
602. Davis W. Carver, b. 1855, 7 mo. 9, d. 1860, 9 mo. 21.

(Benjamin[4], Henry[3], William[2], William[1].)

(153.) Miranda Carver[5]—another daughter of Benjamin Carver and Sarah Kirk, his wife—was born in Plumstead, 1810, 10th month 25; married George Huey, and resided in Lumberville, Solebury Twp, Pa. Both are dead; left one child:

603. John Huey.

(Benjamin[4], Heury[3], William[2], William[1].)

(154.) Mary Carver[5]—another daughter of Benjamin Carver and Sarah Kirk, his wife—was born in Plumstead, 1813, 5th month 28; married William Johnson, 1833, 11th month 23, and died 1847, 8th month 14. Had children:

604. Edward Johnson, b. 1835, 5 mo. 8.
605. George W. Johnson, b. 1841, 12 mo. 12, d. unm.
606. William E. Johnson, b. 1845, 1 mo. 18.
607. Caroline Johnson, b. 1836, 3 mo. 29.
608. Phebe A. Johnson, b. 1839, 11 mo. 11, d. unm. 1859, 7 mo. 1.

(Benjamin[4], Henry[3], William[2], William[1].)

(156.) Elizabeth Carver[5]—another daughter of Benjamin Carver and Sarah Kirk, his wife—was born 1795, 10th month 3; married Abraham Black, a vendue crier, and died leaving children:

609. Jesse Black.
610. Julia Black, d. unm.
611. Sarah C. Black, b. 1818, 3 mo. 15.
612. Henry Black.
613. Benjamin Black.
614. Kirk Black.
615. Elizabeth F. Black, b. 1830, 7 mo. 20.
616. Rebecca J. Black, b. 1832, 11 mo. 14, d. 1835, 10 mo. 9.
617. Eli Black.
618. Mary Black.

(David[4], Rachel[3], William[2], William[1].)

(157) Charles Harrold[5]—a son of David Harrold and Martha Wall, his wife—was born in Tompkins Co., N. Y., 1813, 12th month 22. He studied law under Mason & Torbert, in Springfield, Ohio, and was admitted to practice in 1836. He was a fine scholar and had a valuable library. He was possessed of fifteen hundred acres of land in Fayette Co., Ohio. He was never married and was found dead in his bed in the morning of June 28, 1873, having died of apoplexy.

(David⁴, Rachel³, William², William¹.)

(158.) Alfred Harrold⁵—another son of David and Martha—was born in Ohio, 1815, 5th month 11, and died in August, 1836; not married.

(David⁴, Rachel³, William², William¹.)

(159.) William Harrold⁵—another son of David Harrold and Martha Wall, his wife—was born in Ohio, 1818, 11th month 19. He was a farmer and lived with his father at the Harrold Homestead which contained 3000 acres of land in Clark, Madison, and Fayette Counties, Ohio. He married in June, 1843, Margaret Jones, whose family came from Wales. He died at the Homestead, in Madison Co., Ohio, March 22, 1861. He had eight children, to wit:

619. Marsella Harrold, d. in infancy.
620. Minnie Harrold, d. at about 18 years.
620½. Oliver Harrold, d. young.
621. Alfred Harrold, b. 1844, 8 mo. 6.
622. Maria Harrold.
623. Emma Harrold.
624. Annie Harrold.
625. Seymore Harrold.

Samuel Harrold, the name of the first of the Harrolds of whom we have any record, was born in Normandy, France. He held a lieutenant-colonel's commission in King William's army, and served in several battles in England and Ireland. Among other engagements, he was present and active at the famous Battle of the Boyne in 1690, July 1st (old style), where he lost one of his legs by a cannon ball. For this service in the army, King William gave him a grant of land in County Cavan, Ireland, where he settled, married, and raised one son named William, who, when he was grown, married into a family by the name of Eliott. William had but one child to survive him named Samuel, born in 1728. He came to America at the age of seventeen and married a lady by the name of Russell, by whom he had seven children, five boys and two girls. His wife died in 1777. He afterwards married Rachel Carver, widow of Henry, whose maiden name was Smith; by her he had two children, David and Rebecca (see Nos. 32 and 33, page 3).

(David⁴, Rachel³, William², William¹.)

(160.) Soland Harrold⁵—a son of David Harrold and Martha, his wife—was born in Ohio, and died in infancy.

(David⁴, Rachel³, William², William¹.)

(161.) Caroline Harrold⁵—another daughter of David Harrold and Martha, his wife—was born in Ohio, and died in infancy.

WILLIAM CARVER

(Rebecca⁴, Rachel³, William², William¹.)

(162.) Rachel H. Gillingham⁵—a daughter of Rebecca Harrold and Joseph Gillingham, her husband—was born in the City of Philadelphia, 1803, 4th month, and died in infancy.

(Rebecca⁴, Rachel³, William², William¹.)

(163.) Samuel H. Gillingham⁵—a son of Rebecca Harrold and Joseph Gillingham, her husband—was born in the City of Philadelphia, 1804, 7th month 31; married Lucy L. Eddy in 1826. She died in August, 1836. In 1839, Samuel married his second wife, Louisa H. Hubbs. He died 1854, 2d month 10. His children are three by his first wife and one by his second wife:

626. Fanney E. Gillingham, b. 1827, 10 mo. 4.
627. Joseph E. Gillingham, b. 1830, 7 mo. 5.
628. Lewis H. Gillingham, b. 1836, 7 mo. 3.
629. Frank C. Gillingham, b. 1840, 4 mo. 14, by second wife.

Joseph Gillingham, the father, was born 1780, 8th month 3, in Bucks Co., Pa., of Yeomans Gillingham and Bridget Moon, his wife, and died May 3, 1867, æt. 86 years, 9 months.

(Rebecca⁴, Rachel³, William², William¹.)

(165.) Ann Gillingham⁵—another daughter of Rebecca Harrold and Joseph Gillingham, her husband—was born 1807, 12th month 5; married John F. Gilpin, June 12, 1833, who was born 1796, 11th month 11, and died July 21, 1869, leaving children:

630. Rebecca H. Gilpin, b. 1834, 3 mo. 21.
631. George Gilpin, b. 1838, 12 mo. 21.

(Rebecca⁴, Rachel³, William², William¹.)

(166.) Emmaline L. Gillingham⁵—another daughter of Rebecca Harrold and Joseph Gillingham, her husband—was born 1809, 11th month 11; married Dilworth Buckman, 1842, 10th month 13, and died in Virginia 1877, 1st month 23. Had children:

632. Anna Frances Buckman, b. 1844, 1 mo. 17.
633. Caroline L. Buckman, b. 1841, 1 mo. 31.
634. S. Harrold Buckman, b. 1855, 1 mo. 6.

(Rebecca⁴, Rachel³, William², William¹.)

(167.) Elizabeth Gillingham⁵—another daughter of Rebecca and Joseph—was born 1811, 12th month 20. Died unmarried, 1879, 10th month 12.

(168.) Rebecca Gillingham, b. 1813, 11 mo. 12, d. unm.

(169.) Josephine Gillingham, b. 1816, 3 mo. 3, d. unm.

(170.) Joseph H. Gillingham, born 1818, 8th month 8, unmarried.

(171.) Catharine Oldden Gillingham, born 1820, 11th month 20, unmarried.

(172.) Frances Gillingham, born of Rebecca and Joseph, 1823, 7th month 2, unmarried.

(173.) Caroline Gillingham, born 1825, 9th month 17, of Rebecca and Joseph, unmarried.

(Israel[5], William[4], William[3], William[2], William[1].)
(174.) Frank Morris Carver—a son of Israel Carver and Charity, his wife—married Sarah Blansham of the State of New York, and they reside there.

(Israel[5], William[4], William[3], William[2], William[1].)
(175.) Sarah Carver[6]—a daughter of Joseph Carver and Charity, his wife—was twice married: first, to Samuel Shaw, and had three children by him, two boys and a girl. The girl died and also the father. Sarah then married Henry Boyer, and had one child by him, to wit:

635. William Shaw.
636. Allen Shaw.
637. Daugh Shaw, d. young.
638. Edward Boyer, by second husband.

(Israel[5], William[4], William[3], William[2], William[1].)
(176.) William Carver[6],—another son of Israel Carver and Charity, his wife—married Mary E. McAdams. Had children:

639. Edward E. Carver, m. Hannah Vansant.
640. Mary Emma Carver, d.
641. Charles H. Carver.
642. Elmer E. Carver.

(Israel[5], William[4], William[3], William[2], William.[1])
(177.) David Carver[6]—another son of Israel Carver and Charity, his wife—was twice married: first, to Caroline Stradling, daughter of Samuel of Newtown, Pa.; secondly, to Sarah Richardson of Maryland. He had one child, a son:

643. ———— Carver, b. about 1869.

(178.) Deborah E. Carver—another daughter of Israel Carver and Charity—was born 1835, 9th month 24; married William Lewis, 1857, 11th month 11. Had seven children, to wit:

644. Flora Z. Lewis, b. 1859, 2 mo. 20.
645. Ida M. Lewis, b. 1861, 4 mo. 5, d. 1868, 8 mo. 20.
646. Howard A. Lewis, b. 1863, 6 mo. 1.

647. Fannie S. Lewis, b. 1866, 4 mo. 19.
648. Evan T. Lewis, b. 1868, 12 mo. 12.
649. Sallie W. Lewis, b. 1871, 3 mo. 6.
650. Franklin H. Lewis, b. 1878, 2 mo. 3.

(Israel[5], William[4], William[3], William[2], William[1].)
(179.) Mary Carver[6]—another daughter of Israel Carver and Charity, his wife—married Samuel W. Miller, 1850, 10th month 10, and died 1879, 3d month 13. Had children:

651. Frank Miller, b. 1852, 8 mo. 1.
652. William E. Miller, b. 1857, 10 mo. 16, d. 1865, 7 mo. 26.
653. Carrie Miller, b. 1861, 1 mo. 27.

(Israel[5], William[4], William[3], William[2], William[1].)
(180.) Strickland Carver[6]—another son of Israel Carver, and Charity, his wife—married Asenath White. Had children:

654. Kirk Carver.
655. Mary Carver.
656. Matilda Carver.

(Israel[5], William[4], William[3], William[2], William[1].)
(181.) Lydia Carver[6]—another daughter of Israel Carver and Charity, his wife—married Amos White, son of David, and resides at Furlong in Buckingham Twp., Pa. Have children:

657. Maria White.
658. David White, m. Mary C. Kirk.
659. Mary A. White, m. George Cosner.
660. Sarah White, m. Winfield Large.
661. Elizabeth White.
662. Israel White, d.

(David[5], William[4], William[3], William[2], William[1].)
(182.) Jane G. Carver[6]—a daughter of David P. Carver and Rachel Martendale, his wife—married David Reynolds of Solebury with one child:

663. Mary Ellen Reynolds.

(David[5], William[4], William[3], William[2], William[1].)
(183.) Evelina P. Carver[6]—another daughter of David P. Carver and Rachel Martendale, his wife—died unmarried.

(David[5], William[4], William[3], William[2], William[1].)
(184.) Theodore Carver[6]—a son of David P. Carver and Rachel Martendale, his wife—married Sarah Bodine, daughter of John R., Esq., of Buckingham. Have one child:

664. Harry Carver.

(David[5], William[4], William[3], William[2], William[1].)

(185.) Stephen Carver[6]—another son of David P. Carver and Rachel Martendale, his wife—married, in 1858, Emily E. Keen, who was born 1839, 1st month 13. His children are:

665. Theodore S. Carver.
666. Herbert L. Carver.

Emily E. died in Philadelphia, March 27, 1888, of apoplexy of the heart, æt. 47 years, 2 months, 2 days.

(Miles[5], William[4], William[3], William[2], William[1].)

(186.) Beulah Carver[6]—a daughter of Miles Carver and Ann Martendale, his wife—married Joseph M. Carr of Warminster.

(Miles[5], William[4], William[3], William[2], William[1].)

(187.) Mary Carver[6]—another daughter of Miles Carver and Ann Martendale, his wife—married Stephen K. Doan of Wrightstown Twp. They have one child:

667. Annie K. Doan.

(Miles[5], William[4], William[3], William[2], William[1].)

(188.) Benjamin Watson Carver[6]—a son of Miles Carver and Ann Martendale, his wife—was born in Buckingham and married Harriet Cooper. Have one child:

668. Mary Emma Carver.

(Miles[5], William[4], William[3], William[2], William[1].)

(189.) Thomas Ellwood Carver[6]—another son of Miles Carver and Ann Martendale, his wife—was born in Buckingham Twp; married Julia A. Tomlinson of Bensalem Twp, Pa. They have one child:

669. Elmer Ellsworth Carver.

(Miles[5], William[4], William[3], William[2], William[1].)

(190.) Angelina Carver[6]—another daughter of Miles Carver and Ann Martendale, his wife—married Amos Bennet of Warwick Twp. Have no children.

(Miles[5], William[4], William[3], William[2], William[1].)

(191.) George W. Carver[6]—another son of Miles Carver and Ann Martendale, his wife—was born in Buckingham; married Mary D. Winner. No children.

(Ann[5], William[4], William[3], William[2], William[1].)

(192.) James McDowell[6]—a son of Ann Carver and Samuel McDowell, her husband—married Elizabeth Walton. They reside in Philadelphia. Their children are:

WILLIAM CARVER

670. George McDowell.
671. Henry McDowell.
672. Caroline McDowell.
673. Hannah McDowell.

(Ann[5], William[4], William[3], William[2], William[1].)
(193.) Napoleon McDowell[6]—another son of Ann Carver and Samuel McDowell, her husband—died unmarried.

(194.) Martha McDowell—a daughter of Ann Carver and Samuel McDowell, her husband. Know nothing.

(Henry[5], William[4], William[3], William[2], William[1].)
(195.) William Carver[6]—a son of Major Henry Carver and Catharine Worthington, his wife—died unmarried.

(Henry[5], William[4], William[3], William[2], William[1].)
(196.) Henry Carver[5]—another son of Major Henry Carver and Catharine Worthington, his wife. Know nothing.

(Henry[5], William[4], William[3], William[2], William[1].)
(197.) Margaret Carver[6]—a daughter of Major Henry Carver and Catharine Worthington, his wife—married Reading Miller. Had children:

674. Caroline Miller.
675. Adaline Miller.
676. Kate Miller.

(Henry[5], William[4], William[3], William[2], William[1].)
(198.) Thomas Early Carver[6]—another son of Major Henry Carver and Catharine Worthington, his wife—married, and died leaving one child:

677. Anna Carver.

(199.) Willets Carver—another son of Major Henry Carver and Catharine Worthington, his wife—died young.

(Henry[5], William[4], William[3], William[2], William[1].)
(200). Caroline Carver[6]—another daughter of Major Henry Carver and Catharine Worthington, his wife—married James L. Shaw, son of Josiah of Doylestown Boro. Her children are:

678. Henrietta Shaw.
679. Phebe Shaw.
680. Caroline Shaw.
681. Anna Shaw.
682. James Merritt Shaw.

(Henry⁵, William⁴, William³, William², William¹.)

(201.) Nelson Carver⁶—another son of Major Henry Carver and Catharine Worthington, his wife—died young.

(Henry⁵, William⁴, William³, William², William¹.)

(202.) Ann Eliza Carver⁶—another daughter of Major Henry Carver and Catharine Worthington, his wife—married Chalkly Good, son of Nathan of Solebury. Had no children.

(Henry⁵, William⁴, William³, William², William¹.)

(203.) John Carver⁶—another son of Major Henry Carver and Catharine Worthington, his wife—married Clarinda Collins. Had children:

683. Anna Carver.
684. Clara Carver.
685. George C. Carver.

(204.) Charles Carver—another son of Major Henry Carver and Catharine Worthington, his wife—died young.

(Henry⁵, William⁴, William³, William², William¹.)

(205.) Mary Carver⁶—another daughter of Major Henry Carver and Catharine Worthington, his wife—married George Mitchell. They had one child, but it died almost immediately after birth.

(Henry⁵, William⁴, William³, William², William¹.)

(206.) Kate Carver⁶—another daughter of Major Henry Carver and Catharine Worthington, his wife—married 1852, — month 25, Edwin Middleton. They had children:

686. Clara Middleton, d. in infancy.
687. Henrietta Middleton.
688. Willis Middleton.
689. Merritt Middleton.

(207.) George W. Carver, born of second wife.

(Joseph⁵, William⁴, William³, William², William¹.)

(209.) Eli W. Carver⁶—a son of Joseph Carver and Rebecca White, his wife—was born in Buckingham Twp, 1821, 5th month 25; married Hannah Ann Townsend. Had children:

690. Joseph Carver.
691. William H. Carver.
692. Anna Carver.
693. Mitchell Carver.
694. Elizabeth Carver.
695. Robert W. Carver.

WILLIAM CARVER

(Joseph[5], William[4], William[3], William[2], William[1].)

(208.) Maria Carver[6]—a daughter of Joseph Carver and Rebecca White, his wife—was born in Buckingham, Pa., 1819, 5th month 24; married Oliver Heath, 1853, and had one child:

696. Marietta Heath, m. Lewis De Haven.

(Joseph[5], William[4], William[3], William[2], William[1].)

(210.) Benjamin Carver[6]—another son of Joseph Carver and Rebecca White, his wife—was born 1823, 8th month 12, died 1836, 11th month 4. Unmarried.

(Joseph[5], William[4], William[3], William[2], William[1].)

(211.) Aaron E. Carver[6]—another son of Joseph Carver and Rebecca White, his wife—was born in Buckingham Twp, 1825, 9th month 19; married Letitia McDowell, 1849, 8th month 2, and had children:

697. Ann Rebecca Carver.
698. Stephen S. Carver.
699. Rachel Carver.
700. Ross Carver.
701. Emma Carver.
702. Angelina Carver.

(Joseph[5], William[4], William[3], William[2], William[1].)

(212.) George W. Carver[6]—another son of Joseph Carver and Rebecca White, his wife—was born in Buckingham, 1827, 12th month 11; married. His children are:

703. Hannah Carver.
704. Maria Carver.

(Joseph[5], William[4], William[3], William[2], William[1].)

(213.) Stephen P. Carver[6]—another son of Joseph Carver and Rebecca White, his wife—was born in Buckingham, 1829, 11th month 21, and died 1831, 8th month 25, æt. 1 year, 9 months, 4 days.

(Joseph[5], William[4], William[3], William[2], William[1].)

(214.) Albert W. Carver[6]—another son of Joseph Carver and Rebecca White, his wife—was born in Buckingham, 1831, 10th month 13; married Hannah Seltzer, 1853, 10th month 20. His children are:

705. Maria H. Carver.
706. Laura S. Carver.
707. Lorenzo A. Carver.
708. Ella L. Carver.
709. Harry T. S. Carver.

(Joseph⁵, William⁴, Willtam³, William², William¹.)

(215.) Phebe Ann Carver⁶—another daughter of Joseph Carver and Rebecca White, his wife—was born in Buckingham, 1833, 11th month 11; married William Davis and died 1879, 9th month 10. Had children:

710. George H. Davis.
711. Edward Davis.
712. Joseph A. Davis.
713. Henrietta Davis.

(216.) Rachel Carver—another daughter of Joseph Carver and Rebecca White, his wife—was born in Buckingham, 1835, 10th month 27; married and had two children, who are dead.

(Joseph⁵, William⁴, William³, William², William¹.)

(217.) William Carver⁶—another son of Joseph Carver and Rebecca White, his wife—was born in Buckingham, 1837, 9th month 19; married, and had two children:

714. Albert Carver, d.
715. Wilhelmina Carver, d.

(Joseph⁵, William⁴, William³, William², William¹.)

(218.) Harrison W. Carver⁶—another son of Joseph Carver and Rebecca White, his wife—was born in Buckingham, 1847, 7th month 2; married Mary K. Paist, daughter of Benjamin. She was born 1846, and died 1883, 8th month 15. No children.

(James⁵, William⁴, William³, William², William¹.)

(219.) Alfred S. Carver⁶—a son of James Carver, and Mary Paxson, his wife—was born 1820; married Mary Slutter of Hilltown, 1841, 10th month 7, where he resided. He died 1886, 8th month 7, æt. 66 years, 7 months, 7 days. His children are:

716. Wilhelmina Carver, b. 1842, m. Levi Means, had a daughter, and died in confinement.
717. James Henry Carver.
718. Terissa Carver, m. David Morgan; had a son.

(James⁵, William⁴, William³, William², William¹.)

(220.) Paxson Carver⁶—another son of James Carver and Mary Paxson, his wife—was born 1822, 4th month 11; married Elizabeth R. Ott, 1845, 11th month 6. She was born 1823, 11th month 6. They reside in Solebury. Have children:

719. Nathan C. Carver, b. 1846, 12 mo. 18.
720. Joseph Ott Carver, b. 1848, 10 mo. 2.
721. Addie C. Carver, b. 1851, 1 mo. 11.
722. Emma B. Carver, b. 1853, 1 mo. 15.
723. Susanna O. Carver, b. 1857, 8 mo. 21, d. 1860, 10 mo. 2.

WILLIAM CARVER

724. Hannah K. Carver, b. 1859, 10 mo. 27, d. 1860, 10 mo. 7.
725. Catharine K. Carver, b. 1863, 9 mo. 17.

(James[5], William[4], William[3], William[2], William[1].)

(221.) Harriet Carver[6]—a daughter of James Carver and Mary Paxson, his wife—married John Gunning. They moved to the State of Delaware. She died there about the year 1854. Their children are:

726. Henry Gunning.
727. Alexander Gunning.

(222.) Miles Carver—another son of James and Mary—died in infancy.

(223.) Edwin Carver—another son of James Carver and Tamor Monday, his second wife—not married.

(James[5], William[4], William[3], William[2], William[1].)

(224.) Mary Carver[6]—another daughter of James Carver and second wife—married Septimus White. Had children:

728. Lama White.
729. ———— White.

(James[5], William[4], William[3], William[2], William[1].)

(225.) Hannah Carver[6]—another daughter of James Carver and Tamor Monday, his second wife—married Lewis Kepler residing in Carversville. Have one child:

730. Fred Keppler.

(James[5], William[4], William[3], William[2], William[1].)

(226.) Phebe Carver[6]—another daughter of James Carver and Tamor Monday, his second wife—married Joel Barton. Has children:

731. Ella Barton.
732. Edward Barton.
732½. Emma Barton.
733. James Barton.
734. William Barton.

(James[5], William[4], William[3], William[2], William[1].)

(227.) Nathan Carver[6]—another son of James and Tamor—is not married.

(228.) Henry Carver—another son of James and Tamor, his second wife—married Rebecca Philips and reside in Falls Twp. Have one child:

735. Edward Carver.

(James[5], William[4], William[3], William[2], William[1].)

(229.) Eugene Carver[6]—another son of James Carver and Tamor Monday, his second wife—died in the army in the War of the Rebellion, in 1861. Unmarried.

46 GENEALOGY OF

(James[5], William[4], William[3], William[2], William[1].)

(230.) Frank Carver—another son of James Carver and Tamor Monday, his second wife—was twice married: first, to Ann Lewis; she died, and he then married Sarah Sellers. Had children:

736. Laura Carver.
737. Samuel Carver.

(231.) Charles Carver—another son of James and Tamor, his second wife—died unmarried.

(James[5], William[4], William[3], William[2], William[1].)

(232.) Margaret Carver[6]—another daughter of James Carver and Tamor Monday, his second wife—married William Swartz. Have children:

738. Isabella Swartz.
739. Margaret Swartz.
740. Jane Swartz.

(233.) Kate Carver—another daughter of James and Tamor, died unmarried.

(James[5], William[4], William[3], William[2], William[1].)

(234.) Amanda Carver[6]—another daughter of James Carver and Tamor Monday, his second wife—married, 1873, Charles W. Sickel. Have children:

741. Walter Sickel, b. 1874, 11 mo. 3.
742. Harry Sickel, b. 1877, 5 mo. 8.

(Sarah[5], William[4], William[3], William[2], William[1].)

(235.) Smith Stradling[6]—a son of Sarah Carver and William Stradling—was born 1820, 4th month 23; married Emily H. Graham. Smith died 1879, 1st month 31. Had one child:

743. Nellie Stradling.

(Sarah[5], William[4], William[3], William[2], William[1].)

(236) Mary Stradling[6]—a daughter of Sarah Carver and William Stradling, her husband—was born 1821, 8th month 25; married William Buckman. Have no children.

(Sarah[5], William[4], William[3], William[2], William[1].)

(237.) Hutchinson Stradling[6]—another son of Sarah Carver and William Stradling, her husband—was born 1823, 2d month 17; married Mary Buckman, and went West. Their children are:

744. Anna Stradling.
745. Rachel Stradling.
746. Elizabeth Stradling.

(238.) Miles Stradling, born 1824, 10th month 20—a son of Sarah Carver and William Stradling, her husband—died young.

WILLIAM CARVER

(Sarah[5], William[4], William[3], William[2], William[1].)

(239.) Martha B. Stradling[6]—another daughter of Sarah Carver and William Stradling, her husband—was born 1828, 8th month 12; married 1847, 10th month 7, Jesse Atkinson, son of Samuel. Jesse died 1876, 10th month 7. Have children:

747. Georgiene Atkinson.
748. William S. Atkinson.
749. Stephen K. Atkinson.
750. Sallie S. Atkinson.

(Benjamin[5], William[4], William[3], William[2], William[1].)

(240.) Nathan Carver[6]—a son of Benjamin Carver and Hannah Robinson, her husband—was born 1823, 11th month 27, died 1846, 7th month 13. Not married.

(241.) Miles Carver—another son of Benjamin Carver and Hannah Robinson, his wife—was born 1828, 10th month 19; died 1831, 9th month 10.

(241 ½) Martha B. Carver—a daughter of Benjamin Carver and Hannah Robinson, his wife—was born 1836, 5th month 20; married David Faesi, 1851, 10th month 6. Their children died in infancy.

(Benjamin[5], William[4], William[3], William[2], William[1].)

(242.) Smith Carver[6]—another son of Benjamin Carver and Hannah Robinson, his wife—was born 1839, 2d month 19; married 1866, 9th month 12, Sarah E. Montgomery, and died 1877, 11th month 23. His children are:

751. Clara L. Carver, b. 1876, 9 mo. 18.
752. Hannah M. Carver, b. 1869, 6 mo. 29.
753. Mattie B. Carver, b. 1872, 4 mo. 21.

(Benjamin[5], William[4], William[3], William[2], William[1].)

(243.) Benjamin Carver, Jr.[6]—another son of Benjamin Carver and Hannah Robinson, his wife—was born 1842, 2d month 4; married A. Baum in 1860. Their children all died in infancy.

(Esther[5], William[4], William[3], William[2], William[1].)

(244.) Eliza Ann McDowell[6]—daughter of Esther Carver and William McDowell, her husband—was born 1811, 4th month 10; married William T. Beans, 1836, 7th month 17, and died in Crelaski Co., Indiana, 1850, 10th month 30, æt. 39 years, 6 months, 20 days. Know nothing of their children.

(Esther[5], William[4], William[3], William[2], William[1].)

(245.) Hannah McDowell[6]—another daughter of Esther Carver and William McDowell, her husband—married Joel Carver, his second wife, 1836, 5th month 3. They had one child:

754. Angelina Carver, b. 1842, 6 mo. 9, d. 1842, 7 mo. 6.

(Esther[5], William[4], William[3], William[2], William[1].)

(246.) George McDowell[6]—a son of Esther Carver and William McDowell, her husband—married Amanda Mathews, and has children, viz.:

755. A. Caroline McDowell.
756. Esther McDowell.
757. William H. McDowell.
758. Kinsey McDowell.
759. George McDowell.

(247.) Joseph McDowell—another son of Esther Carver and William McDowell, her husband—married. Had no children.

(248.) William McDowell — another son of Esther Carver and William McDowell, her husband—was born 1818, 12th month 18; married 1842, 3d month 23, Eleanor Duer, born 1816, 6th month 23. William died 1877, 2d month 28, æt. 58 years, 2 months, 10 days. He had the following children:

760. Anna M. McDowell, b. 1843, 7 mo. 7.
761. Hannah L. McDowell, b. 1845, 9 mo. 4.
762. Clarissa McDowell, b. 1849, 4 mo. 7, d. 1850, 8 mo. 22.

(Esther[5], William[4], William[3], William[2], William[1].)

(249.) Robert McDowell[6] — another son of Esther Carver and William McDowell, her husband—was born 1818, 12th month 18, being a twin of William. Married Catharine Neff. Had children:

763. William McDowell, d.
764. Jennie McDowell, d.
765. Lettie McDowell.

(Esther[5], William[4], William[3], William[2], William[1].)

(250.) Charles M. Blaker[6]—another son of Esther Carver and Mahlon Blaker, her second husband—was born 1824, 8th month 12; married Levinia Lair, 1851, 11th month 29. Her children are:

766. Angelina C. Blaker, b. 1853, 4 mo. 13, d. 1853, 9 mo. 11.
767. Hannah Ellen Blaker, b. 1855, 12 mo. 14.
768. William Windfield Blaker, b. 1858, 7th month 18.

WILLIAM CARVER

(Joseph[5], Joseph[4], William[3], William[2], William[1].)

(251.) **William K. Carver**[6]—a son of Joseph Carver, Esq., and Cynthia Kirk, his wife—was born in Buckingham Twp, 1816, 5th month 27; married Sarah Phillips, 1850, 1st month 31. His wife, Sarah, died 1864, 6th month 25. Had children:

769. Joseph P. Carver, b. 1852, 4 mo. 26.
770. Adella Carver, b. 1856, 8 mo. 26.
771. William K. Carver, Jr., b. 1860, 2 mo. 28, d. 1864, 5 mo. 26.

(Joseph[5], William[4], William[3], William[2], William[1].)

(252.) **Wilson J. Carver**[6]—another son of Joseph Carver, Esq., and Cynthia Kirk, his wife—was born in Buckingham in 1818; married Elizabeth F. Philips of Newtown in 1839. She died in 1870, 11th month 25. His second wife was Catharine Stephenson of Philadelphia; married 1875, 5th month. No children by her. Wilson died in Philadelphia, 1885, 4th month 24, in his 67th year. Had children:

772. Mary Emily Carver, b. 1842, 6 mo.
773. Roxanna F. Carver, b. 1844, 6 mo.
774. J. Harper Carver.
775. William A. Carver.
776. Elizabeth R. Carver.

(Joseph[5], William[4], William[3], William[2], William[1].)

(253.) **Jesse Carver**[6]—another son of Joseph Carver, Esq., and Cynthia Kirk, his wife—was born in 1820; married Jane C. Woodman of Norristown, Pa., 1843, 2d month 9. Had children:

777. Dr. Wilson C. Carver, b. 1844, 2 mo. 10.
778. Maggie R. Carver, b. 1846, 3 mo. 17.
779. Isabella F. Carver, b. 1848, 5 mo. 27.
780. Joseph B. Carver, M.D., b. 1857, 4 mo. 1.
781. Walton W. Carver, b. 1860, 2 mo. 27.

Jane, the mother, died 1880, 10th month 22.

(Joseph[5], William[4], William[3], William[2], William[1].)

(254.) **Joseph Carver, Jr.**[6]—another son of Joseph Carver, Esq., and Cynthia Kirk, his wife—was born 1822, 6th month 9; married Rebecca F. Woodman, 1852, 3d month 10, and died at Jacksonville, Ill., 1881, 2d 25, æt. 58 years, 8 months, 16 days. Has children:

782. Mary Ellen Carver, b. 1854, 7 mo. 13.
783. Linda A. Carver, b. 1858, 10 mo. 26.
784. Edward H. Carver, b. 1863, 2 mo. 11.
785. Elizabeth G. Carver, b. 1825, 6 mo. 1.

GENEALOGY OF

(Joseph⁵, William⁴, William³, William², William¹.)

(255.) Mary E. Carver⁶—a daughter of Joseph Carver, Esq., and Cynthia Kirk, his wife—was born in Buckingham Twp, Pa., 1825, 9th month 9. She and Edward Woodman were married 1858, 3d month 22. She died 1863, 5th month 27, leaving one child:

786. William C. Woodman, b. 1859, 1 mo. 7.

(Joseph⁵, William⁴, William³, William², William¹.)

(256.) Elizabeth K. Carver⁶—another daughter of Joseph Carver, Esq., and Cynthia Kirk, his wife—was born in Buckingham in 1828, 3d month 3; she and Joseph J. Greer, son of Jefferson of Plumstead, were married 1853, 1st month 12. They had one child:

787. Alice J. Greer, b. 1853, 11 mo. 23.

(Jesse⁵, Joseph⁴, William³, William², William¹.)

(257.) C. Harrison Carver⁶—a son of Jesse P. Carver and Elizabeth Tucker, his wife—was twice married: first, to Hannah Fell, by whom he had one child; secondly, to Elizabeth Roberts. He had a daughter by her. He resides in Lambertville, and is a merchant.

788. ——— Carver.
789. Hannah Carver.

(258.) Lewis T. Carver—another son of Jesse P. Carver and Elizabeth Tucker, his wife—is not married.

(Jesse⁵, Joseph⁴, William³, William², William¹.)

(259.) John J. Carver⁶—another son of Jesse P. Carver and Elizabeth Tucker, his wife—died at the Insane Hospital at Harrisburg about September 5, 1881.

(260.) Banner Taylor—a son of Sarah Bradshaw and Joseph Taylor, her husband—went to Canada.

(261.) Watson W. Taylor—another son of Sarah Bradshaw and Joseph Taylor, her husband—went to Canada.

(David⁵, Elizabeth⁴, William³, William², William¹.)

(262.) Seriphina Taylor⁶—a daughter of Sarah Bradshaw and Joseph Taylor, her husband—married William Worthington of Buckingham Twp, whose will is proven in Will Book No. 20, page 277, December 31, 1878. He left no widow, but children, to wit:

790. Spencer T. Worthington.
791. Martha Worthington.

WILLIAM CARVER

(263.) Mary Taylor—another daughter of Sarah Bradshaw and Joseph Taylor, her husband—married ——— Welding.

(266.) Minerva S. Paist—a daughter of Sidney Bradshaw and Jonathan Paist, her husband—was born in 1806; married George W. Scott in 1839. They had one child:

792. Wilhelmina Minerva Scott.

(267.) David Bradshaw Paist—a son of Sidney Bradshaw and Jonathan Paist, her husband—was born 1808; married Mary Ann West in 1831, and died at his residence in Lesbon, Linn Co., Iowa, 1886, 4th month 10. His children are:

793. Josephine T. Paist, b. in 1835.
794. Samueline Paist, b. in 1837.
795. Jonathan T. Paist, b. in 1839.
796. Sarah E. Paist, b. in 1842.
797. Mary A. Paist, b. in 1843.
798. Charles E. Paist.
799. Edward H. Paist.
800. Monroe B. Paist.
801. Harvey S. Paist, d.

(Sidney[5], Elizabeth[4], William[3], William[2], William[1].)

(268.) J. Monroe Paist[6]—another son of Sidney Bradshaw and Jonathan Paist, her husband—was born in 1819; married Elizabeth Connard, 1850, 2d month 7. Their children are:

802. Alice M. Paist, b. 1850, 11 mo. 21.
803. Andrew C. Paist, b. 1855, 2 mo. 14.
804. Jonathan E. Paist, b. 1857, 9 mo. 30.
805. Mary R. Paist, b. 1860, 9 mo. 18.
806. Joseph H. Paist, b. 1862, 12 mo. 1.

(269.) Eliza A. Paist—another daughter of Sidney Bradshaw and Jonathan Paist, her husband—was born 1810. Died.

(270.) David Heston Bradshaw—a son of David Bradshaw, Jr., and Melicent Large, his wife—married Mary Stull of Trenton, New Jersey, in 1862. They have one child:

807. Melicent Bradshaw.

(271.) Joseph Bradshaw—another son of David Bradshaw, Jr., and Melicent Large, his wife—married Margaret McDonald in 1849. Have children:

808. Ellen Bradshaw, b. 1850.
809. Henry Bradshaw, b. 1853.

(272.) Lewis W. Bradshaw—another son of David Bradshaw and Melicent Large, his wife—married Amanda Campbell in 1857. Have children:

810. Melicent Bradshaw, b. 1858.
811. Sallie Bradshaw, b. 1861.

(273.) Seraphina T. Bradshaw—a daughter of David Bradshaw and Melicent Large, his wife—married William Ellis, February 6, 1851. Have children:

812. Franklin B. Ellis, b. 1852, 10 mo. 8.
813. J. Watson Ellis, b. 1855, 11 mo. 28.
814. Charles W. Ellis, b. 1860, 3 mo. 28.
815. Albro L. Ellis, b. 1862, 3 mo. 12.
816. Bessie Ellis, b. 1869, 6 mo. 7.

(274.) Rebecca Bradshaw—another daughter of David Bradshaw and Melicent Large, his wife—was twice married: first, to Samuel Scott of Hartsville, Bucks Co., Pa., 1858, 6th month 27. Had children:

817. George W. Scott, b. 1859, 8 mo. 21, d. 1872, 11 mo. 8.
818. William S. Scott, b. 1861, 4 mo. 5.
819. Edward B. Scott, b. 1863, 1 mo. 8.
820. David Heston Scott, b. 1864, 5 mo. 14.
821. S. Milton Scott, b. 1869, 5 mo. 22.
822. Lizzie S. Scott, b. 1872, 7 mo. 5.

Samuel Scott, the first husband, died 1772, 4th month 5.
Rebecca's second husband was Dr. Isaiah Micheneor, V.S. They were married 1877, 6th month 14. No children.

(275.) Anna M. Bradshaw—another daughter of David Bradshaw and Melicent Large—died unmarried.

(276.) Mary Elizabeth Bradshaw—another daughter of David Bradshaw and Melicent Large, his wife—married Solomon Laurance 1869, 12th month 3. Have children:

823. Dwight C. Laurance, b. 1870, 12 mo. 27.
824. David Edson Laurance, b. 1872, 8 mo. 5.
825. Anna M. Laurance, b. 1874, 2 mo. 23.
826. Edith Laurance, b. 1876, 2 mo. 5.
827. Maggie K. Laurance, b. 1878, 5 mo. 28.

(277.) Ruth Ann Meredith—a daughter of Ruth Bradshaw and Moses Meredith, her husband—married Martin Lippincott of Buckingham Twp. Had children:

WILLIAM CARVER

828. Wilson Lippincott.
829. Watson Lippincott.
830. Anna B. Lippincott.
831. Ellsworth Lippincott.
832. Martin Lippincott.
833. Ruth Lippincott.

(278.) Anna Maria Meredith—a daughter of Ruth Bardshaw and Moses Meredith, her husband—married. Know nothing.

(279.) Watson Meredith—a son of Ruth Bradshaw and Moses Meredith, her husband—died young.

(Elizabeth[6], Elizabeth[4], William[3], William[2], William[1].)
(280.) John Roland Linburg[6]—a son of Elizabeth Bradshaw and Sylvester Linburg, her husband—married ——— Walker. They are both dead, leaving one child:

834. John Linburg.

(281.) Howard Linburg—another son of Elizabeth Bradshaw and Sylvester Linburg, her husband—died.

(Elizabeth[6], Elizabeth[4], William[3], William[2], William[1].)
(282.) Benjamin Morris Linburg[6]—another son of Elizabeth Bradshaw and Sylvester Linburg, her husband—married Loretta Skelton, daughter of James L. of Solebury, deceased. Their children are:

835. Gertrude Linburg.
835½. Jeremiah Linburg.
836. Mary Linburg.
837. Florence Linburg.
838. Edna Linburg.
839. Theodore Linburg.

(Elizabeth[6], Elizabeth[4], William[3], William[2], Wiliam[1].)
(283.) Ruth Ann Linburg[6]—a daughter of Elizabeth Bradshaw and Sylvester Linburg, her husband—married Mordecai Pearson of Solebury, but they now reside in Northampton Twp, Bucks Co. He is dead. Have children:

840. John L. Pearson.
841. Clayton Pearson.
842. Sallie Pearson.
843. Filmore Pearson.
844. Mary Emma Pearson.
845. Morris Pearson.
846. Anna Pearson.
847. Watson Linburg Pearson.
848. A. Curtain Pearson.
849. Maggie Pearson.

(William[5], Mary[4], William[3], William[2], William[1].)

(284.) Rebecca Kirk[6]—the oldest child of William Kirk and Phebe Malone—was born in Buckingham, 1812, 1st month 20; married Amos M. Carver, son of John. Died leaving seven children:

850. Comley Carver, b. 1835, 10 mo. 14.
851. Mahlon Carver, b. 1838, 3 mo. 13, unm.
852. William K. Carver, b. 1841, 1 mo. 8, unm.
853. Mary Carver, b. 1844, 2 mo. 6.
854. Kesih Carver, b. 1846, 10 mo. 5.
855. Mercy Carver, b. 1849, 5 mo. 3.
856. Ellen K. Carver, b. 1853, 6 mo. 5.

(William[5], Mary[4], William[3], William[2], William[1].)

(285.) Spencer W. Kirk[6]—a son of William Kirk and Phebe Malone, his wife—was born in Buckingham Twp, Pa.; married Lydia Kirk, daughter of Isaac C., and died in Philadelphia, leaving children:

857. Lorenzo Kirk.
858. Ella Kirk.

(William[5], Mary[4], William[3], William[2], William[1].)

(286.) Stephen Smith Kirk[6]—another son of William Kirk and Phebe Malone, his wife—was born in Buckingham; married Angelina H. Trego. Have one child:

859. John T. Kirk.

(William[5], Mary[4], William[3], William[2], William[1].)

(287.) John M. Kirk[6]—another son of William Kirk and Phebe Malone, his wife—was born in Buckingham, and was twice married: first, to Mary Vasey, daughter of Joel; had three children by her. She died and he secondly married Hulda Fell, daughter of Eli, Sr. Had one child by her:

860. Emma Kirk.
861. Pierson Kirk.
862. Edwin J. Kirk.
863. Harry Kirk, by second wife.

(William[5], Mary[4], William[3], William[2], William[1].)

(288.) William Mitchel Kirk[6]—another son of William Kirk and Phebe Malone, his wife—was born in Buckingham; married Ellen Johnson. Has one child:

864. Johnson Kirk.

(William[6], Mary[4], William[3], William[2], William[1].)

(289.) Nelson Kirk[6]—another son of William Kirk and Phebe Johnson, his wife—married Marjary Ann Carver, daughter of John, and died in December, 1873. Have children:

865. William John Kirk.
866. Mary C. Kirk.
867. Lindora Kirk.
868. Allen Kirk.
869. Stephen Kirk.

(William[5], Mary[4], William[3], William[2], William[1].)

(290.) Albert Kirk[6]—another son of William Kirk and Phebe Johnson—married Eliza Hartley. Have no children.

(291.) Charles Kirk[6]—another son of William and Phebe—not married.

(292.) Mary Ellen Kirk[6]—another daughter of William and Phebe—died young.

(293.) Evelina Doan—a daughter of Sarah Kirk and Benjamin Doan, her husband—married Kinsey Harvey. Have children:

869¼. Edward Harvey, d. unm.
869½. Benjamin Harvey, d. unm.
870. Harrison Harvey, d. unm.
871. William D. Harvey.
872. Matthias Harvey.
873. Sarah Jane Harvey.
874. Kinsey Harvey.
875. Theodore Harvey.
876. David Harvey, d. in infancy.

(Sarah[5], Mary[4], William[3], William[2], William[1].)

(294.) John K. Doan[6]—a son of Sarah Kirk and Benjamin Doan, her husband—married Sarah Pearson. Have one child:

877. Augustus W. Doan.

(Sarah[5], Mary[4], William[3], William[2], William[1].)

(295.) Eleazer Doan[6]—another son of Sarah Kirk and Benjamin Doan, her husband—married Martha Thomas. No children.

(Sarah[5], Mary[4], William[3], William[2], William[1].)

(296.) Amos Doan[6]—another son of Sarah Kirk and Benjamin Doan, her husband—married Elizabeth Paist. Have children:

878. Edward C. Doan.
879. Eleazer T. Doan.
880. B. Frank Doan.
881. Henry Doan.

(Sarah[5], Mary[4], William[3], William[2], William[1].)

(297.) William K. Doan[6]—another son of Sarah Kirk and Benjamin Doan, her husband—was twice married: first, to Elizabeth Corson and had four children. She died and he married secondly Hannah Gilbert and had five children, to wit:

882. Benjamin E. Doan.
883. Hannah K. Doan.
884. Sarah Doan.
885. Martha Doan.
886. Miranda Doan.
887. Horace Doan.
888. Warran Doan.
889. Josephine Doan.
890. Flora Doan.

(Sarah[5], Mary[4], William[3], William[2], William[1].)

(298.) Benjamin C. Doan[6]—another son of Sarah Kirk and Benjamin Doan, her husband—married Mary Kean. Had children:

891. Charles Doan, d. in infancy
892. Benjamin Doan.

(Sarah[5], Mary[4], William[3], William[2], William[1].)

(299.) Stephen K. Doan[6]—another son of Sarah Kirk and Benjamin Doan, her husband—married Mary Carver. Had childred:

893. Anne K. Doan.
894. Theodore J. Doan.
895. Miranda K. Doan.

(Sarah[5], Mary[4], William[3], William[2], William[1].)

(300.) Theodore J. Doan[6]—another son of Sarah Kirk and Benjamin Doan, her husband—married Ellen Kirk. Had children:

896. Adella Doan.
897. Clara M. Doan.

(Sarah[5], Mary[4], William[3], William[2], William[1].)

(301.) Mary Doan[6]—another daughter of Sarah Kirk and Benjamin Doan, her husband—married John Cooper, Esq. Have one child:

898. Stephen K. Cooper.

(Sarah[5], Mary[4], William[3], William[2], William[1].)

(302.) Sarah S. Doan[6]—another daughter of Sarah Kirk and Benjamin Doan, her husband—was twice married; first, to Benjamin Eastburn, by whom he had his children; secondly, to James M. Vandegrift. His children are:

899. George L. Eastburn.
900. Isabella Easturn.

(Sarah[5], Mary[4], William[3], William[2], William[1].)
(303.) Miranda K. Doan[6]—another daughter of Sarah Kirk and Benjamin Doan, her husband—married John H. Baker. No children.

(304.) Randolph K. Betts—a son of Mary Kirk and John Betts, Jr., her husband—was born 1813, 1st month 27, died 1814, 1st month 3.

(305.) Mary Kirk Betts—a daughter of Mary Kirk and John Betts, Jr., her husband—was born 1815, 5th month 19, died 1820, 11th month 20.

(Mary[5], Mary[4], William[3], William[2], William[1].)
(306.) Sarah Ann Betts[6]—another daughter of Mary Kirk and John Betts, Jr., her husband—was born 1816, 10th month 14; married Thomas Ely. Their children are:
901. Mary Anna Ely.
902. Watson Ely.
903. Kizzie Ely.
904. Hannah Ely.
905. Isaac Ely.
906. Emma Ely.

(Mary[5], Mary[4], William[3], William[2], William[1].)
(307.) Letitia Anderson Betts[6]—another daughter of Mary Kirk and John Betts, Jr., her husband—was born 1821, 11th month 8; married Chapman Kirk. Had children:
907. Theodore Kirk.
908. Chapman Kirk.

(Mary[5], Mary[4], William[3], William[2], William[1].)
(308.) Sampson Carey Betts[6]—another son of Mary Kirk and John Betts, Jr., her husband—was born 1825, 6th month 23; married, first, Caroline Carver, and had but one child. She died and he then married Mary Warner, 1855, 5th month 30. His child is:
909. Simpson Lorenzo Betts, d. in his 6th year.

(John[5], Mary[4], William[3], William[2], William[1].)
(309.) John Wilson Kirk[6]—a son of John Kirk and Rachel Kirk, his wife—was born in Buckingham; married Julia Van Tilburg, and have children:
910. Edward Kirk.
911. Franklin Kirk.
912. Elvina Kirk.

GENEALOGY OF

(310.) Joseph Comley Kirk—another son of John and Rachel—not married.

(John[5], Mary[4], William[3], William[2], William[1].)
(311.) Thomas Henry Kirk[6]—another son of John Kirk and Rachel Kirk, his wife—married Amanda Walton. Has children:

913. Walter Kirk.
914. Elmer W. Kirk.

(John[5], Mary[4], William[3], William[2], William[1].)
(312.) Stephen L. Kirk[6]—another son of John Kirk and Rachel Kirk, his wife—married, first, Hannah Atkinson, by whom he had his children. His second wife was Anne Lough. Children are:

915. Mary Kirk.
916. Rachel Kirk.
917. Clinton Kirk.

(313.) Watson W. Kirk—a son of Isaac C. Kirk and Eliza Coates, his wife—was born in Buckingham Twp, Pa., 1821, 9th month 15; married Hannah Corson. No children.

(314.) Maria L. Kirk—a daughter of Isaac C. Kirk and Eliza Coates, his wife—was born in Buckingham, Pa., 1826, 1st month 4; married Isaac P. Corson. Had children:

918. Sarah E. Corson.
919. Edward Corson.

(Isaac[5], Mary[4], William[3], William[2], William[1].)
(315.) Mary Jane Kirk[6]—another daughter of Isaac C. Kirk and Eliza Coates, his wife—was born in Buckingham, 1827, 12th month 2; married Edward Armitage, son of Henry of Solebury, 1852, 12th month 28. Had one child:

920. Sallie M. Armitage, b. 1853, 10 mo. 23.

(Isaac[5], Mary[4], William[3], William[2], William[1].)
(317.) Anna L. Kirk[6]—another daughter of Isaac C. Kirk and Eliza, his wife—was born in Buckingham 1835, 6th month 22; married Emmor Walton and resides in Philadelphia. Children are:

921. Watson W. Walton.
922. William C. Walton.
923. Rachel K. Walton.
924. Laura K. Walton.

(Cornelius[5], Joseph[4], Joseph[3], William[2], William[1].)

(318) Rebecca V. Carver[6]—a daughter of Cornelius Carver and Mary Martendell, his wife—was born about 1814; married Aaron Walton. He died about 1876, leaving one child:

925. Louisa M. Walton.

(Cornelius[5], Joseph[4], Joseph[3], William[2], William[1].)

(319.) Sarah Ann Carver[6]—another daughter of Cornelius Carver and Mary Martendell, his wife—was born about 1815, and married, first, Charles M. Lee. They had one child. He died and she afterwards married Benjamin B. Buckman. She died at Newtown, Bucks Co., Pa., 1884, 3d month 23, æt. 69 years. Her children are:

926. William Wallace Lee, d. unm.
927. Malcolm A. Buckman, b. 1855, 10th mo. 2.

(320.) Derrick K. Carver—a son of Garret V. Carver and Elizabeth Krusen, his wife—was born in Northampton, Twp, Pa., 1815, 1st month 23; married Mary Scudder 1840, 2nd month 19, and died at Trenton, N. J., 1875, 1st month 10. Had children:

928. Gustavius A. Carver, b. 1842, 3 mo. 9.
929. Joseph Victor Carver, b. 1845, 6 mo. 23.

(321.) Joseph V. Carver—another son of Garret V. Carver and Elizabeth Krusen, his wife—was born 1816, 5th month 15; married Martha Woodward of Montgomery Co., Pa., in 1840. Had by her a daughter. His wife died in 1842 and he moved to Bradford Co., Pa.; married his second wife, Margaret Rhoades of Luzerne, Pa., and resides now at Cheshire, New Haven, Conn. His children are:

930. Angelina Carver, b. by first wife.
931. Emma Carver, b. 1850, 11 mo. 6.
932. William R. Carver, b. 1854, 4 mo. 2.
933. Edgar J. Carver, b. 1861, 4 mo. 25, unm.
934. Henry D. Carver, b. 1864, 9 mo. 10, unm.
935. Frank D. Carver, b. 1866, 10 mo. 15, unm.

(Garret[5], Joseph[4], Joseph[3], William[2], William[1].)

(322.) Mary Carver[6]—a daughter of Garret V. Carver and Elizabeth Krusen, his wife—was born in Northampton Twp; married Jacob V. Cornell, and died 1872, 7th month. Jacob then married his second wife, Isabella, but had no children by her. He died in 1878. His will is dated 1878, 8th month 2; proven 1878, 10th month 1, in Will Book No. 20, page 248. His executors were his sons, James and Albert. His children are:

936. Emma Ann Cornell, m. James Wesley Hellings, no children.
937. Mary Jane Cornell.
938. Albert Cornell.
939. Harry R. Cornell.
940. William Cornell.
941. Margaret Cornell.
942. Franklin Cornell.

(Mary[5], Joseph[4], Joseph[3], William[2], William[1].)

(323.) Thomas W. Bye[6]—a son of Mary V. Carver and Thomas Bye, Jr., her husband—was born in Buckingham, Pa., 1807, 12th month 20; married Rachel Hart, and died intestate, 1865, 12th month 21. He left a widow and children:

942½. John Hart Bye.
943. Sarah K. Bye.
944. Mary V. Bye, unm.
945. Anna R. Bye.
946. Franklin P. Bye, d. unm.

(Mary[5], Joseph[4], Joseph[3], William[2], William[1].)

(324.) Joseph C. Bye[6]—another son of Mary V. Carver and Thomas Bye, Jr., her husband—was born in Buckingham, Bucks Co., Pa., 1810, 6th month 6; married Rachel Seaman, and died at Atlantic City, N. J., in December, 1872. His will bears date June 18, 1872, and was proven in Doylestown in Will Book No. 18, page 482. Had children:

947. Lorenzo Seaman Bye.
948. Pleasant Monroe Bye.
949. Josephine Bye.

(325.) Allen R. Bye—another son of Mary V. Carver and Thomas Bye, Jr., her husband—was born in Buckingham, 1813, 9th month 6; married Margaret Felty, and died in Solebury in February, 1878. He left children:

950. Allen Bye, Jr.
951. Nathan F. Bye.
952. Elizabeth F. Bye.

(Joel⁵, Joseph⁴, Joseph³, William², William¹.)

(326) **Anna G. Carver⁶**—a daughter of Joel Carver and Lydia Gill, his first wife—married Richard Everett, deceased. Had children:

953. Martha Everett.
954. Alice Everett.
955. Randolph Everett.

(Joel⁵, Joseph⁴, Joseph³, William², William¹.)

(327.) **Angelina Carver⁶**—Another daughter of Joel Carver and Hannah McDowell, his second wife—was born 1842, 6th month 9, died 1842, 7th month 6.

(Joseph⁵, Joel⁴, Joseph³, William², William¹.)

(328.) **Jane Carver⁶**—a daughter of Joseph Carver and Ann Carey, his wife—was born in Northampton Twp, Bucks Co., 1798, 11th month 2; married Benjamin Hibbs in 1818, 11th month 2. Their children are:

956. Joseph C. Hibbs, b. 1819.
957. Sarah Ann Hibbs.
958. Hannah Hibbs, unm.

(Robert⁵, Joel⁴, Joseph³, William², William¹.)

(329.) **Joseph Carver⁶**—a son of Robert Carver and Mary Smith, his wife—was born in Northampton Twp, Pa., and married Mary Cherry. He moved to Hancock Co., Ohio. His children are:

959. John Carver.
960. Robert Carver.
961. Mary Carver.
962. Marjary Carver.
963. Martha Carver.
964. Elizabeth Carver.
965. Ellen Carver.
966. William Carver, d. unm.

(Robert⁵, Joel⁴, Joseph³, William², William¹.)

(330.) **Smith Carver⁶**—another son of Robert Carver and Mary Smith, his wife—was born in Northampton Twp, Bucks Co.; married Barbary Hillborn, and moved to Hancock Co., Ohio. Had children:

967. William Carver.
968. James Carver.
969. Sarah Carver.

(Robert⁵, Joel⁴, Joseph³, William², William¹.)

(331.) **Elizabeth Carver⁶**—a daughter of Robert Carver and Mary Smith, his wife—was born in Northampton Twp, Bucks Co., Pa.; married Mahlon Smith of Wrightstown. Had children:

970. Henry Q. Smith.
971. Lewis Smith.

(332.) Joel Carver—another son of Robert Carver and Mary Smith, his wife—was born in Northampton Twp about 1811. He was not married, and died at Penn's Park, Wrightstown, 1884, 12th month 17, æt. 73 years.

(333.) Samuel Carver—another son of Robert and Mary—died unmarried.

(Robert[5], Joel[4], Joseph[3], William[2], William[1].)
(334.) William Carver[6]—another son of Robert Carver and Mary Smith, his wife—was married to Edith Croasdale. Has children:

972. Agnes Carver.
973. Lizzie Carver.
974. Mary Carver.

(Robert[5], Joel[4], Joseph[3], William[2], William[1].)
(335.) Ann Carver[6]—another daughter of Robert Carver and Mary Smith, his wife—married Robert Beans, of Northampton Twp, Bucks Co., Pa. Their children are:

975. Anna Mary Beans, d. young.
976. Carrie Beans,
977. Annie E. Beans.
978. Mary C. Beans.
979. Alice Beans.

(Robert[5], Joel[4], Joseph[3], William[2], William[1].)
(336.) Mary Carver[6]—another daughter of Robert Carver and Mary Smith, his wife—married Carlile Smith of Wrightstown Twp, Pa. Have children:

980. Martha Smith.
981. William Smith.

(Robert[5], Joel[4], Joseph[3], William[2], William[1].)
(337.) John Carver[6]—another son of Robert Carver and Mary Smith, his wife—married Mercy Doan, and lived in Solebury Twp, Bucks Co., Pa. His second wife was ———— Beal. His children are by first wife:

982. Joseph Carver.
983. Mary Carver.
984. Cynthia Carver.

(Robert[5], Joel[4], Joseph[3], William[2], William[1].)
(338.) Hannah Carver[6]—a daughter of Robert Carver and Mary Smith—never married.

(339.) Jane Carver[6]—a daughter of Robert Carver and Mary Smith—never married.

WILLIAM CARVER

(Ann⁵, Joel⁴, Joseph³, William², William¹.)

(340.) John Lloyd⁶—a son of Ann Carver and Abraham Lloyd, her first husband—was born 1809, 2nd month 16, and married Amanda M. Morris, daughter of Enos of Newtown Boro, before he was 18 years old. He had two children by her before he was 21, when she died. He died in the Borough of Doylestown, Pa., 1885, 4th month 20, in the evening, æt. 76 years, 1 month, 23 days. He had children:

985. Enos Morris Lloyd, Attorney-at-Law, b. 1827, July 10.
986. Henry C. Lloyd, M.D., b. 1829.

(Joel⁵, Joel⁴, Joseph³, William², William¹.)

(341.) Alfred Carver⁶—a son of Joel Carver and Ann Smith, his wife—was born in Northampton Twp; married Jane Lefferts, and died in December, 1866, leaving children:

987. Maria V. Carver.
988. Edwin Carver.
989. John Carver.

(Joel⁵, Joel⁴, Joseph³, William², William¹.)

(342.) Euphemia V. Carver⁶—a daughter of Joel Carver and Ann Smith, his wife—was born in Northampton Twp; married John K. Torbert, who died in the spring of 1875. Their children are:

990. Henry M. Torbert.
991. Maria V. Torbert.
992. Margaret Torbert.
993. Alfred Torbert.

(343.) Garret Carver—another son of Joel Carver and Ann Smith, his wife—was born in Northampton Twp; married and died, leaving children:

994. Harriet Maria Carver.
995. Joseph Addis Carver.

(344.) Joel Hobensack—a son of Hannah Carver and George Hobensack, her husband—was born in Northampton Twp; married and moved to Marion Co., Ohio. Had children:

996. John Hobensack.
997. George Hobensack.

Hannah⁵, Joel⁴, Joseph³, William², William¹.)

(345.) John Hobensack⁶—a son of Hannah Carver and George Hobensack, her husband—was born in Northampton Twp, Pa.; married Lucella Norris. Had children:

998. James B. Hobensack, M.D.
999. Emma R. Hobensack.

(Hannah[5], Joel[4], Joseph[3], William[2], William[1].)

(346.) George Hobensack[6]—another son of Hannah Carver and George Hobensack, her husband—married and had children:

1000. Ann Hobensack.
1001. Ella Hobensack.

(Hannah[5], Joel[4], Joseph[3], William[2], William[1].)

(347.) Ann Hobensack[6]—a daughter of Hannah Carver and George Hobensack, her husband—was born in Northampton Twp; married Incus Rhoades. Had children:

1002. George Rhoades.
1003. John Rhoades.

(John[5], John[4], Joseph[3], William[2], William[1].)

(348.) John J. Carver[6]—a son of Joseph Carver and Hannah Lovett, his wife—was born in Buckingham; married Margaret Black and died in 1870, 10th month 5. Margaret died in 1888. Their children are:

1004. Enos B. Carver.
1005. John M. Carver.
1006. Emmer Carver.
1007. Clemens C. Carver.
1008. Walter C. Carver.
1009. Henry S. Carver.
1010. Hannah Ann Carver.
1011. Cynthia Carver.
1012. Anna Malissa Carver.

(Joseph[5], John[4], Joseph[3], William[2], William[1].)

(349.) Samuel L. Carver[6]—another son of Joseph Carver and Hannah Lovett, his wife—married Mary Ann McKinstry, died in Buckingham 1877, 6th month 2. Had children:

1013. Anderson Carver.
1014. Chapman M. Carver.
1015. Walter Carver.
1016. Emily Carver.

(Joseph[5], John[4], Joseph[3], William[2], William[1].)

(350.) James Carver[6]—another son of Joseph Carver and Hannah Lovett, his wife—was born 1814, 6th month 6; married Louisa Hamilton, daughter of Benjamin, 1834, 6th month 14, and died in Buckingham 1864, 11th month 2. Children:

1017. Samuel H. Carver.
1018. Loretta Carver.
1019. Ellen Carver.

(Joseph[5], John[4], Joseph[3], William[2], William[1].)

(351.) Joseph Carver[6]—another son of Joseph Carver and Hannah Lovett, his wife—married Rachel Bailey, and died in Virginia during the War of the Rebellion, about 1863. Leaving children:

1020. Sarah Ann Carver.
1021. Ellwood Carver.
1022. Warren Carver.

(352.) William Carver—another son of Joseph Carver and Hannah Lovett, his wife—married Elmina Black. His children are:

1023. Lafayette Carver.
1024. Amy Carver.

(353.) Clemens Carver—a son of William and Elmina—died young.

(354.) Hannah Carver—another daughter of Joseph Carver and Hannah Lovett, his wife—was born in Buckingnam, 1810, 6th month 4; married William R. Kirk, Esq., 1831, 11th month 3. William was a son of John and Jane Kirk of Solebury, Bucks Co., Pa. They came from Ireland when young. Had children:

1025. Samuel Kirk.
1026. William Kirk.
1027. Margaret Kirk.
1028. John Kirk.
1029. Mary Ellen Rirk.

(355.) Audrey Carver—another daughter of Joseph Carver and Hannah Lovett, his wife—was born in Buckingham; married Thomas Baily, and died about 1846, leaving one child:

1030. Edward Baily.

(Joseph[5], John[4], Joseph[3], William[2], William[1].)

(356.) Mary Ann Carver[6]—another daughter of Joseph Carver and Hannah Lovett, his wife—was born in Buckingham 1831, 7th month 26; married H. Morris Cosner, 1854, 4th month 6. Their children are:

1031. Audrey Cosner, b. 1857, 7 mo.
1032. Mary H. Cosner, b. 1859.
1033. Jesse Cosner, b. 1866, 10 mo.
1034. Horatio M. Cosner, b. 1869, 7 mo.
1035. Thomas Cosner, b. 1872, 3 mo.
1036. Joseph Cosner, b. 1873, 9 mo.

(Isaac⁵, Joseph⁴, Joseph³, William², William¹.)

(357.) George W. Carver⁶—a son of Isaac Carver and Sarah Martendale, his wife—was born 1810, 10th month 11; married Mary Ann Carey, 1835, 11th month 20, and resides in West Chester, Pa. Children:

1037. Albina C. Carver, b. 1837, 10 mo. 18, unm.
1038. Isaac Carey Carver, b. 1839, 8 mo. 3.
1039. George Ross Carver, b. 1842, 4 mo. 13, m. Sallie E. Tomlinson.
1040. Henry Nelson Carver, b. 1844, 5 mo. 19.
1041. Sarah Jane Carver, b. 1846, 8 mo. 11.
1042. Mary Ellen Carver, b. 1848, 8 mo. 10.
1043. Miranda Caroline Carver, b. 1851, 2 mo. 14.
1044. William Kirk Carver, b. 1853, 9 mo 1.
1045. Ermina Virginia Carver, b. 1856, 3 mo. 27.
1046. Lewis Hains Carver, b. 1859, 3 mo. 11.

(358.) Mary Ann Carver—a daughter of Eli Carver and Mary Dunlap, his wife—died unmarried.

(359.) John Carver—a son of Eli and Mary—died childless.

(Eli⁵, John⁴, Joseph³, William², William¹.)

(360.) Charles Franklin Carver⁶—was born of Eli Carver and Mary Dunlap, his wife. He was twice married: first, to Phebe Skelton, daughter of John of Solebury; second, to Elizabeth Hamilton Poulton, daughter of Samuel of Plumstead, by Rev. S. T. Thompson, at St. Mary's, Pa., September 1, 1880. She died before he did. He died at The Cross Keys, near Doylestown Boro, Pa., 1889, 9th month 3. Childless.

(361.) Joseph Carver—a son of Eli and Mary—died childless.

(362.) James Carver—another son of Eli and Mary—died childless.

(Eli⁵, John⁴, Joseph³, William², William¹.)

(363.) Elizabeth A. Carver⁶—a daughter of Eli Carver and Mary Dunlap, his wife—was born in Buckingham 1821, 8th month 25; married, 1849, 4th month 15, Henry Williams of Montgomery, Pa. Rev. Henry S. Gilroy officiated. Their children are:

1047. Anna Williams, b. 1850, 2 mo. 23, d. 1852, 6 mo. 22.
1048. Henry Williams, b. 1852, 11 mo. 7.
1049. Charles F. Williams, b. 1856, 4 mo. 30.
1050. Mary C. Williams, b. 1860, 10 mo. 20, unm.
1051. Annie Williams, b. 1864, 7 mo. 24, unm.

(364.) Maria Carver—another daughter of Eli and Mary—died childless.

WILLIAM CARVER

(John[5], John[4], Joseph[3], William[2], William[1].)

(365.) John Carver[6]—a son of John Carver and Mary Martendale, his wife—married Mary E. Howell in 1853. Had children:

1052. Sarah H. Carver, b. 1853.
1053. Harrison E. Carver, b. 1855.
1054. Richard M. Carver, b. 1857.

(366.) Amos M. Carver—another son of John Carver and Mary Martendale, his wife—was born in Buckingham 1813, 10th month 24; married in 1835, 1st month, Rebecca Kirk, who was born 1812, 1st month 20, by whom he had his children. She died in 1880, 7th month 23. He married, secondly, Mrs. Mary Howell of Solebury, 1881, 12th month. They had seven children (see No. 284): Comley Carver, Mahlon Carver, William K. Carver, Mary Carver, Kesiah Carver, Mercy Carver, Ellen K. Carver.

(367.) Jesse M. Carver—another son of John Carver and Mary Martendale, his wife—was born in Buckingham, Bucks Co., Pa., 1810, 3d month 21; married, 1838, 8th month 28, Sarah Watson Lewis, daughter of Thomas of Plumstead. They moved to Illinois in 1851, and she died there in Pre-emption, 1886, 5th month 11, æt. 76 years, 1 month, 20 days. Their children are:

1055. Reading Carver.
1056. Watson Carver.
1057. Letitia Carver.
1058. Marshall Carver.
1059. Thomas Carver.
1060. Edward Carver.
1061. Winfield Carver.
1062. Marietta Carver.

Jesse M. Carver, the father, was born in Buckingham Twp, Bucks Co., Pa., and died in Pre-emption, Mercer Co., Illinois, July 16, 1892, in the 77th year of his age.

"Mrs. Sarah Watson Lewis Carver died at the residence of her
"husband, Jesse M. Carver, in Pre-emption, Illinois, on May 11, 1886,
"aged 76 years, 1 month, 20 days. Mrs. Carver was born in Bucks Co.,
"Pa., March 21, 1810. She was married to her now bereaved husband
"on August 28, 1838, and with him went to Illinois in 1851. She was
"the mother of eight children: six sons and two daughters, all of whom are
"living and all settled in life. Mrs. Carver was a descendant of the Fox and
"Ellicott families, who were Quakers, in which faith she lived and died.
"She was a good wife and mother and enjoyed the respect and esteem of
"the neighbors. Her funeral was held in the M. E. Church, May 13. She
"was laid at rest in the Pre-emption Cemetery."

(John[5], John[4], Joseph[3], William[2], William[1].)

(368.) Adin Carver[6]—another son of John Carver and Mary Martendale, his wife—was born in Buckingham in 1830; married Sarah M. Howell in 1850, and had the following children:

1063. Charles H. Carver, b. 1851.
1064. Mary A. Carver, b. 1854.
1065. Eseck H. Carver, b. 1856.
1066. Sallie J. Carver, b. 1858.
1067. Ida V. Carver, b. 1861, m. Dr. E. A. Horland in 1893.
1068. Laura M. Carver, b. 1871.

(369.) Yardley Carver—another son of John Carver and Mary Martendale, his wife—was born in Buckingham; married Frances Hughes, and died leaving children:

1069. Howard Carver.
1070. Phebe Carver.

(370.) Oliver Carver—another son of John Carver and Mary Martendale, his wife—was born in Buckingham; married Sarah Hughes. Children are:

1071. George Carver, d. unm.
1072. Mary T. Carver, b. 1855.
1073. Roxanna Carver, b. 1857.
1074. Alonzo L. Carver, b. 1860, had a son, Orville Ray Carver.
1075. H. Ellsworth Carver, b. 1866.

(371.) Wilson Carver—another son of John Carver and Mary Martendale, his wife—was born in Buckingham; married Beulah Van Horn. His children are:

1076. Amos Carver.
1077. Eva Carver.
1078. Beulah Carver, d. unm.

(372.) Maria Carver—another daughter of John Carver and Mary Martendale, his wife—married John Lambert. His children are:

1079. Matilda Lambert.
1080. William Lambert.
1081. Abigail Lambert.
1082. Mary E. Lambert.
1083. Lucretia Lambert.
1084. Margery Lambert.

WILLIAM CARVER

(373.) Keziah Carver—another daughter of John Carver and Mary Martendale, his wife—married Allen Trego in 1830. Had children:

1085. Wilson Trego, d. young.
1086. Watson D. Trego.
1087. Mary E. Trego.

(374.) Caroline Carver—another daughter of John Carver and Mary Martendale, his wife—was born in Buckingham; married Simpson Carey Betts in 1869, and died leaving one child:

1088. Lorenzo Betts.

(375.) Mary Carver—another daughter of John Carver and Mary Martendale, his wife—was born in Buckingham; married John Warner. One child:

1089. Charles H. Warner.

(376.) Cynthia Carver—another daughter of John Carver and Mary Martendale, his wife—was born in Buckingham; married Edward Worthington, now deceased. Had children:

1090. Martha C. Worthington.
1091. John J. Worthington.
1092. Mary Ellen Worthington.
1093. Keziah Worthington.
1094. Sarah A. Worthington.
1095. Silas Worthington.
1096. Henry Worthington.
1097. Edward Worthington.
1098. Cynthia Worthington.

(377.) Margery Ann Carver—another daughter of John Carver and Mary Martendale, his wife—was born in Buckingham; married Nelson Kirk, who died in December, 1873. Had children:

1099. William John Kirk.
1100. Mary C. Kirk.
1101. Lindora Kirk.
1102. Allen Kirk.
1103. Stephen Kirk.

GENEALOGY OF

(John⁵, John⁴, Joseph³, William², William¹.)

(378.) Rebecca Carver⁶—another daughter of John Carver and Mary Martendale, his wife—was born in Buckingham, and was twice married: first, to Isaiah B. Terry and had two children. On the 8th of November, 1861, he presented a petition to the Court of Common Pleas of Bucks Co. for a subpœna in divorce. They were divorced September 19, 1862. She then married Joseph Yates. Her children are:

1104. Sarah J. Terry, by first husband.
1105. Maranda Terry, by first husband.
1106. William Yates.
1107. Mary Yates.
1108. Elizabeth Yates.
1109. Edith Yates.
1110. Isabella Yates.
1111. Margaret Yates.
1112. Edward Yates.
1113. Laura Yates.
1114. Ella Yates.

(Martha⁵, John⁴, Joseph³, William², William¹.)

(380.) Nellie Erving⁶—a daughter of Martha Carver and Jesse Erving—was born in Chester Co., Pa. Jesse was Martha's first husband.

(381.) Harriet Walton—daughter of Martha Carver and John Walton, her second husband—was born in Chester Co., Pa.

(382.) John Walton—a son of Martha Carver and John Walton, her second husband—was born in Chester Co., Pa.

(383.) Amy Walton—another daughter of Martha Carver and John Walton, her second husband—was born in Chester Co., Pa.

(384.) Mahlon Gilbert—a son of Phebe Carver and Samuel Gilbert, her husband—was born on Thursday, 1810, 5th month 10, died 1849, 8th month 11, unmarried.

(385.) George W. Gilbert—another son of Phebe Carver and Samuel Gilbert, her husband—was born Tuesday, 1812, 8th month 25, and has been married three times: first, to Eliza Gwinn, had four children by her; secondly, to Debbie Logan, had six children by her; thirdly, to Anna Young. He died suddenly at Norristown, Pa., on Sunday, 1886, 6th month 22, æt. 71 years, 9 months, 26 days. His children are:

1115. Matilda Gilbert. ⎫
1116. Evelina Gilbert.   ⎬ By first wife.
1117. Theodore Gilbert. ⎪
1118. George Gilbert.   ⎭

WILLIAM CARVER

1119. Daniel Gilbert.
1120. Elwood Gilbert.
1121. Harriet Gilbert.
1122. Mary Gilbert.
1123. Phebe Gilbert.
1124. Elizabeth Gilbert.

} By second wife.

Matilda, George, Phebe, and Elizabeth died in infancy.

(386.) Lydia Ann Gilbert—a daughter of Phebe Carver and Samuel Gilbert, her husband—was born Monday, 1814, 11th month 28; married to John Ward on Wednesday, 1837, 4th month 5, by Rev. William Maul of Hatborough. Her children are:

1125. Andrew Ward, b. Wednesday, 1838, 5 mo. 30, d. on Monday.
1126. Watson Tomlinson Ward, b. Thursday, 1840, 4 mo. 2.
1127. Emily Ann Ward, b. Monday, 1842, 9 mo. 5, d. 1858, 1 mo. 30, Sunday.
1128. Phebe Catharine Ward, b. 1846, 9 mo. 25, d. 1847, 11 mo. 1, Monday.
1129. Amos Addis Ward, b. 1853, 1 mo. 15.

(387.) Jonathan Gilbert—another son of Phebe Carver and Samuel Gilbert, her husband—was born on Sunday, 1816, 11th month 10, died 1861, unmarried.

(388.) David Gilbert—another son of Phebe Carver and Samuel Gilbert, her husband—was born on Friday, 1819, 10th month 15, died 1821, 9th month 28.

(Phebe[5], John[4], Joseph[3], William[2], William[1].)

(389.) John Gilbert[6]—another son of Phebe Carver and Samuel Gilbert, her husband—was born Thursday, 1821, 11th month 8; married Mary Ann Wallace, 1845, 2nd month 15, and died in 1853. His children are:

1130. Edward M. Gilbert, b. 1846, 4 mo. 10.
1131. Ann M. Gilbert, b. 1849, 1 mo. 27.

Mary Ann, the mother, died at Norristown, Pa., 1886, 11th month 23, æt. 72 years.

(Phebe[5], John[4], Joseph[3], William[2], William[1].)

(390.) Rebecca Gilbert[6]—another daughter of Phebe Carver and Samuel Gilbert, her husband—was born Thursday, 1824, 1st month 7; married Joseph Evans, 1845, 1st month. Her children are:

1132. John Howard Evans, b. 1846, 1 mo.
1133. Henry L. Evans, b. 1848, 8 mo.
1134. Ann Evans, b. 1850, 9 mo.
1135. Augusta Evans, b. 1852, 8 mo.
1136. Agnes Evans, b. 1854, 8 mo., d. in 1875.
1137. Emily Ann Evans, b. 1857, 3 mo., d.
1138. J. Newton Evans, b. 1859, 5 mo.
1139. Heston Evans, b. 1866, 5 mo.

(Phebe[5], John[4], Joseph[3], William[2], William[1].)

(391.) Howard Gilbert[6]—another son of Phebe Carver and Samuel Gilbert, her husband—was born on Wednesday, 1826, 7th month 26, and was twice married: first, to Euphemia Titus, 1852, 10th month 12, they had one child. The mother died and he married Elizabeth Williams, and died 1868, 4th month 9. His children are:

1140. Howard Gilbert, b. 1853, 8 mo. 15, d. at 5 mo.
1141. Nina M. Gilbert, b. 1851, 12 mo. 12.
1142. Emma Jane Gilbert, b. 1860, 11 mo. 15.
1143. Florence O. Gilbert, b. 1862, 6 mo. 21.
1144. Bessie Mary Gilbert, b. 1864, 12 mo. 9.
1145. John N. Gilbert, b. 1868, 6 mo. 15.

(Phebe[5], John[4], Joseph[3], William[2], Wiliam[1].)

(392.) Asa Comley Gilbert[6]—another son of Phebe Carver and Samuel Gilbert, her husband—was born on Friday, 1828, 10th month 17, and has been three times married. Know nothing more.

(Phebe[5], John[4], Joseph[3], William[2], William[1].)

(393.) Agnes C. Gilbert[6]—another daughter of Phebe Carver and Samuel Gilbert, her husband—was born on Friday, 1828, 10th month 17. A twin with Asa, born one hour before him. She and John Richard Clemens were married by Rev. William Barnes, on Fifth Street below Girard Avenue, on Sunday evening, 1853, 7th month 30. John Richard Clemens was born Thursday, 1821, 9th month 13, near Friends' Meeting House, Radnor, Delaware Co., Pa. Their children are:

1146. John Richard Clemens, Jr., b. Saturday, 1857, 10 mo. 30.
1147. Mary Agnes Clemens, b. Monday, 1859, 3 mo. 10, d. 1865, 10 mo. 13.
1148. Anna A. Clemens, b. Saturday, 1867, 2 mo. 17.

WILLIAM CARVER

(394.) Joseph Haines—a son of Mary Carver and Reuben Haines—know nothing.

(395.) Annie Haines—a daughter of Mary Carver and Reuben Haines—know nothing.

(396.) Margaret Haines—another daughter of Mary Carver and Reuben Haines—know nothing.

(Amy[5], John[4], Joseph[3], William[2], William[1].)

(397.) John Carver Addis[6]—a son of Amy Carver and Amos Addis, her husband—was born 1815, 10th month 8; married 1844, 10th month 23, Martha Ramsey Thomas, born 1822, 2nd month 27, and died 1882, 9th month 3. John died 1878, 12th month 21. Had children:

1149. John Clarkson Addis, b. 1845, 7 mo. 14.
1150. Amos Addis, b. 1847, 9 mo. 21, d. 1850, 8 mo. 14.
1151. Snowden Addis, b. 1850, 9 mo. 6, d. 1851, 7 mo. 12.
1152. George F. Addis, b. 1851, 10 mo. 19, d. 1883, 3 mo 27.
1153. Jonathan W. Addis, b. 1853, 8 mo. 25, d. 1855, 11 mo. 30.
1154. Robert Addis, b. 1856, 12 mo. 23.
1155. Herman S. Addis, b. 1859, 9 mo. 23.

(Amy[5], John[4], Joseph[3], William[2], William[1].)

(398.) Ellen Addis[6]—a daughter of Amy Carver and Amos Addis, her husband—was born 1812, 11th month; married Jocob Krewsen, and died 1841, 3d month, and her husband died 1862, 5th month. Their children are:

1156. Amos Addis Krewsen.
1157. Helen Krewsen.

(Amy[5], John[4], Joseph[3], William[2], William[1].)

(399.) Isaac Clarkson Addis[6]—another son of Amy Carver and Amos Addis, her husband—was born 1819, 9th month 30; was twice married: first, to Elizabeth H. Yerkes in 1845; had three children by her. She died 1872, 8th month. His second wife was Amy H. Yerkes, daughter of Elias. His children are:

1158. Amy Addis, b. 1848, 5 mo.
1159. Anna Addis, b. 1852.
1160. Howard Addis, b. 1856.

GENEALOGY OF

(Amy[5], John[4], Joseph[3], William[2], William[1].)

(400.) Eliza Ann Addis[6]—anothdr daughter of Amy Carver and Amos Addis, her husband—was born 1824, 9th month; married Elias P. Hall, son of Elias of Southampton, in 1845. She died 1858, 11th month, and he died in the Army of the Rebellion. Children:

1161. Mary F. Hall, d. 1867.
1162. Amy M. Hall.
1163. Sallie G. Hall.
1164. Elizabeth Hall.
1165. Albert J. Hall.

(Amy[5], John[4], Joseph[3], William[2], William[1].)

(401.) Mary Hutchinson Addis[6]—another daughter of Amy Carver and Amos Addis, her husband—was born 1830, 10th month; married 1851, 11th month 20, Jonathan Warner Martindell, and lived at Pineville, Bucks Co., Pa., and had the following children:

1166. Thomas H. Martindell, b. 1852, 10 mo. 5, d. 1857, 7 mo. 24.
1167. Miles M. Martindell, b. 1853, 9 mo. 29.
1168. Annie Addis Martindell, b. 1855, 9 mo. 29.
1169. Amos Addis Martindell, b. 1857, 3 mo. 19.
1170. Edwin W. Martindell, b. 1859, 1 mo. 3.
1171. Isaiah M. Martindell, b. 1860, 12 mo. 25.
1172. Benjamin C. Martindell, b. 1862, 10 mo. 5, d. 1863, 9 mo. 12.
1173. Jonathan Warner Martindell, b. 1865, 2 mo. 6.
1174. Mary M. Martindell, 1867, b. 2 mo. 22.
1175. Emma J. Martindell, b. 1872, 8 mo. 27.

(401 ½.) Isabella Short—a daughter of Ann Carver and John Short—was born in Cecil Co., Md., died unmarried.

(402.) William Short—a son of Ann Carver and John Short, her husband—was born in Cecil Co., Md., died unmarried.

(403.) John Short—another son of Ann Carver, and John Short, her husband—was born in Cecil Co., Md., died unmarried.

(Ann[5], John[4], Joseph[3], William[2], William[1].)

(404.) Robert L. Houpt[6]—a son of Ann Carver and Samuel Houpt, her second husband—was born in Chester Co., Pa., 1829, 10th month 1; married Mary Anderson. Had one child, to wit:

1176. Jacob Houpt, b. 1851.

(Ann[5], John[4], Joseph[3], William[2], William[1].)

(405.) Ann Eliza Houpt[6]—a daughter of Ann Carver and Samuel Houpt, her second husband—was born in Chester Co., Pa., 1832, 5th month 9; married Samuel D. Lingerman, 1847, 2nd month 9, of Moreland, Philadelphia. Her children are:

1177. George Courtney Lingerman, b. 1847, 11 mo. 28.
1178. Richard Carver Lingerman, b. 1851, 2 mo. 9, d. 1872, 12 mo.
1179. Mary Ellen Lingerman, b. 1853, 11 mo. 4, d. 1853, 11 mo. 18.
1180. Harry Alphonso Lingerman, b. 1855, 10 mo. 24, d. 1861, 12 mo. 31.
1181. Anna Clara Lingerman, b. 1858, 2 mo. 24.
1182. Jennie Ward Lingerman, b. 1861, 11 mo. 6, d. 1862, 1 mo. 8.

(Joseph[5], Ruth[4], Joseph[3], William[2], William[1].)

(406.) Harvey Terry[6]—a son of Joseph C. Terry and Mary Vansant, his wife—was born in Wrightstown Twp, Bucks Co., Pa., in 1821, 2nd month. He was a merchant in Philadelphia; quit business there in 1854. Opened a private bank in Milwaukee in 1858; closed it successfully in 1862. Went to the army in 1862, as a cotton buyer, till 1864. Returned with a fortune; invested largely in Southern State Bonds and Bank Bills to hundreds of thousands of dollars and lost heavily. In 1872-3 was admitted to the Bar and practiced law in the Supreme Court of Georgia, and in 1875 was admitted to the Supreme Court of the United States at Washington, D. C.; but he has now retired from practice, and resides in New York City. He was married in 1848, at Philadelphia, to Sarah G. Garson, but has no children.

(Joseph[5], Ruth[4], Joseph[3], William[2], William[1].)

(407.) Isaiah B. Terry[6]—a son of Joseph C. Terry and Mary Vansant, his wife—was born in Wrightstown Twp, Bucks Co., Pa., in 1823; married Rebecca Carver, daughter of John and Mary Martendale. They had two children, and were then divorced at September Court, 1862. Their children are:

1183. Sarah Jane Terry.
1184. Miranda Terry.

(Joseph[5], Ruth[4], Joseph[3], William[2], William[1].)

(408.) Eliza Jane Terry[6]—a daughter of Joseph C. Terry and Mary Vansant, his wife—was born in Wrightstown, Bucks Co., Pa., 1827, 3d month 6; married Gideon Erwin. Had children:

1185. William Erwin.
1186. John Erwin.
1187. George Erwin.
1188. Gideon Erwin.

(Joseph[5], Ruth[4], Joseph[3], William[2], William[1].)

(409.) Hannah A. Terry[6]—a daughter of Joseph C. Terry and Mary Vansant, his wife—was born in Wrightstown, 1826, 6th month 8; married Timothy Ely. Has children:

1189. Harvey T. Ely.
1190. George Franklin Ely.
1191. Anna Mary Ely.
1192. Walter Ely, d. young.
1193. Elmer Ellsworth Ely.

(Joseph[5], Ruth[4], Joseph[3], William[2], William[1].)

(410.) John V. Terry[6]—another son of Joseph C. Terry and Mary Vansant, his wife—was born 1831, 8th month at Wrightstown, Bucks Co., Pa., and was twice married: first, to Harriet Brown, daughter of Robert of Chester Co., Pa., 1857, 11th month. She died in 1859, leaving one child who died in his 12th year. Secondly, to H. Kate Evans, daughter of John Watson Evans of Newark, Del., in 1866. Had children:

1194. Edwin B. Terry, by first wife, d. in his 12th year.
1195. Walter Evans Terry.
1196. J. Herman Terry.
1197. John Watson Terry, } twins, d. in infancy.
1198. Harvey B. Terry,

(411.) Mary Ann Terry[6]—another daughter of Joseph C. Terry and Mary Vansant, his wife—was born in Wrightstown, Pa., 1834, 10th month, not married.

(Joseph[5], Ruth[4], Joseph[3], William[2], William[1].)

(412.) Oliver T. Terry[6]—another son of Joseph C. Terry and Mary Vansant, his wife—was born in Wrightstown, Pa., 1837; married Harriet Young. Have children:

1199. Catharine Terry.
1200. Annie Terry.
1201. Oliver T. Terry.

(413.) Caroline Terry[6]—another daughter of Joseph C. and Mary Vansant—died young.

(414.) Mary Ann Beans—a daughter of Martha Terry and John Beans, her husband—was born 1819, 11th month 22, and died 1838, 9th month 24. No children.

(Martha[5], Ruth[4], Joseph[3], William[2], William[1].)

(415.) Sarah T. Beans[6]—another daughter of Martha Terry and John Beans, her husband—was born 1821, 11th month 3; married Rev. William K.

WILLIAM CARVER

Goentner, 1839, 3d month 26. He died at Hatborough, Pa., 1886, 2nd month 16, in his 72nd year. Their children are:

1202. Mary Ann Beans Goentner, b. 1840, 7 mo. 23, d. 1848, 2 mo. 1.
1203. Martha Goentner, b. 1843, 1 mo. 10, d. 1848, 1 mo. 26.
1204. Maria Amanda Goentner, b. 1845, 1 mo. 10.
1205. William Krider Goentner, b. 1847, 6 mo. 27, d. 1847, 8 mo. 26, } twins.
1206. John Beans Goentner, b. 1847, 6 mo. 27,
1207. Charles Terry Goentner, D.V.S., b. 1852, 2 mo. 2.
1208. Mannie Eliza Goentner, b. 1849, 8 mo. 27.
1209. Sara Wilhelmina Goentner, b. 1854, 5 mo. 19. Teacher.
1210. William Krider Goentner, b. 1857, 3 mo. 7.
1211. Katherina Goentner, b. 1959, 9 mo. 6.
1212. Angela Goentner, b. 1862, 4 mo. 26.
1213. Martha Ella Goentner, b. 1863, 8 mo. 26.

(Martha[5], Ruth[4], Joseph[3], William[2], William[1].)

(416.) Amanda Beans[6]—another daughter of Martha Terry and John Beans, her husband—was born 1823, 11th month 9; married Rev. Mahlon H. Sisty, 1841, 11th month 23, and died 1860, 4th month 1. Their children are:

1214. Martha Eliza Sisty, b. 1843, 6 mo. 30.
1215. John Beans Sisty, b. 1845, 8 mo. 26.
1216. Mary Amanda Sisty, b. 1847, d.
1217. Anna Augusta Sisty, b. 1850, 8 mo. 26.

(417.) Eliza L. Beans—another daughter of Martha Terry and John Beans, her husband—was born 1829, 9th month 24.

(James[5], Ruth[4], Joseph[3], William[2], William[1].)

(418.) Joshua V. Terry[6]—a son of James Terry and Aletha Baily, his wife—was born 1822, 1st month 11, and married Anneta Gross. Had children:

1218. William Terry.
1219. Robert B. Terry.
1220. Alonzo Terry.
1221. Frank Terry.

(419.) Martha Terry—a daughter of James Terry and Aletha Baily, his wife—was born 1825, 11th month 10, and married Benjamin Chew. Had children:

1222. James Chew.
1223. Benjamin Chew.
1224. Kate Chew.

GENEALOGY OF

(420.) William Terry—another son of James Terry and Aletha Baily, his wife—was born 1828, 9th month 12, and was twice married: first, to Margaret Dougherty, by whom he had his children; secondly, to Mary Bates, no children by her.

1225. Annie Terry.
1226. Margaret Terry.
1227. William Terry.

(James[5], Ruth[4], Joseph[3], William[2], William[1].)

(421.) Samuel B. Terry[6]—a twin of William, born of James Terry and Aletha Baily, his wife—was born 1828, 9th month 12, and was twice married: first, to Margaret Shaffer, by whom he had one child; secondly, to Mary Holt. His children:

1228. Elizabeth Terry.
1229. Sarah Terry.
1230. Laura Terry.
1231. John Terry.

(422.) James M. Terry—another son of James Terry and Aletha Baily, his wife—was born 1831, 3d month 19, died at 5 years old.

(James[5], Ruth[4], Joseph[3], William[2], William[1].)

(423.) Aletha W. Terry[6]—another daughter of James Terry and Aletha Baily, his wife—was born 1833, 4th month 21, and married John Wood. Has children:

1232. John Wood.
1233. Aletha Wood.

(424.) Edward Terry[6]—another son of James Terry and Aletha Wood, his wife—was born 1835, 6th month 19, and married Mary Ogleby. No children.

(425.) Wesley B. Terry[6]—born of James Terry and Aletha Baily, 1838, 1st month 26, and died one month after birth.

(James[5], Ruth[4], Joseph[3], William[2], William[1].)

(426.) Mary V. Terry[6]—of James Terry and Aletha Baily—was born 1839, 8th month 3; married Augustus Large. Had children:

1234. Frank Large.
1235. Clayton Large.

(427.) Rachel Ann Terry—of James Terry and Aletha Baily—was born 1841, 8th month 11; married Jesse Smith, and died at the age of 23. No children.

WILLIAM CARVER

(428.) Ruth Terry—of James Terry and Aletha Baily—was born 1844, 1st month 20, and died 18 months after.

(James[5], Ruth[4], Joseph[3], William[2], William[1].)
(429.) Sarah Amanda Terry[6]—another daughter of James Terry and Amanda Reed, second wife—was born 1848, 12th month 28, and married 1868, 9th month 16, Andrew J. Hall. Had children:

1236. Elmira Hall, b. 1871.
1237. Ruth Hall, b. 1875.

(430.) Margaret Emma Terry—of James and Amanda Reed, his wife—was born 1851, 2nd month 5, and died æt. 4 years.

(431.) Isaac Kline Terry—born of James and Amanda, his second wife, and died 1 year after.

(432.) Joseph Carver Terry—born of James and Amanda, his second wife, 1856, 6th month 1, and died 6 weeks after.

(John[5], Martha[4], Joseph[3], William[2], William[1].)
(433.) Charles M. Price[6]—a son of John Price, Esq., and Elizabeth Kirk, his wife—married Susan Rich; died in 1872. Had children:

1238. John Price.
1239. William Price.

(John[5], Martha[4], Joseph[3], William[2], William[1].)
(434.) Kirk J. Price[6]—another son of John Price, Esq., and Elizabeth Kirk, his wife—married Sarah Brown, daughter of Samuel of Plumstead. Had children:

1240. John Price, thrown from a horse in Philadelphia and killed.
1241. Esther Price, m. ——— Taylor; no children.

(John[5], Martha[4], Joseph[3], William[2], William[1].)
(435.) Stephen K. Price[6]—another son of John Price, Esq., and Elizabeth Kirk, his wife—married Rebecca Carey, daughter of Thomas of Solebury. Had child:

1242. Henry Price.

(436.) Sarah Price—a daughter of John Price, Esq., and Elizabeth Kirk, his wife—married.

(John[5], Martha[4], Joseph[3], William[2], William[1].)
(437.) Smith Price[6]—another son of John Price, Esq., and Elizabeth Kirk, his wife—married Henrietta Opp, daughter of Valentine Opp of Doylestown Boro, and died 1868. Had child:

1243. Valentine Price.

(John⁵, Martha⁴, Joseph³, William², William¹.)

(438.) Preston Price⁶—another son of John Price, Esq., and Elizabeth Kirk, his wife—married ———— Good, daughter of Nathan of Solebury. Preston died in 1880, 7th month 25. Had children:

1244. Edward Price.
1245. Ellen Price.
1246. Oliver Price.

(John⁵, Martha⁴, Joseph³, William², William¹.)

(439.) Hannah Price⁶—another daughter of John Price, Esq., and Elizabeth Kirk, his wife—married Eleazer C. Church, a printer, 1847, 12th month, of Newtown Boro. Her children are:

1247. William Church.
1248. Watson Church.
1249. Mary Church.
1250. Harry Church.
1251. Annie Church.

(John⁵, Martha⁴, Joseph³, William², William¹.)

(440.) John N. Price⁶—another son of John Price, Esq., and Elizabeth Kirk, his wife—married, and died in the Boro of Doylestown, 1886, 9th month 8. His children are:

1252. Sidney Price.
1253. Samuel G. Price.
1254. Edwin Price.
1255. Mary Price.

(Martha⁵, William⁴, Joseph³, William², William¹.)

(441.) William C. Pool⁶—a son of Martha Carver and William Pool, her husband—was born 1801, 11th month 13; married Maria Thompson, daughter of Hugh of Wrightstown, and died intestate in 1855. Charles Thompson, Esq., of Wrightstown was his administrator. Had children:

1256. Mary Pool, b. 1830, 10 mo. 16, d. 1831, 3 mo. 7.
1257. Hugh Thompson Pool, b. 1831, 12 mo. 21, d. 1850, 2 mo 19.
1258. Martha Pool, b. 1836, 2 mo. 22, d. 1836, 7 mo. 29.
1259. Edward Q. Pool, b. 1834, 3 mo. 9.
1260. John T. Pool, b. 1837, 7 mo. 2.
1261. William Pool, b. 1840, 2 mo. 13, d. 1864, 11 mo. 24.
1262. Samuel T. Pool, b. 1842, 1 mo. 16.
1263. Anna Elizabeth Pool, b. 1844, 5 mo. 5.
1264. George C. Pool, b. 1846, 11 mo 11.
1265. Thomas T. Pool, b. 1848, 3 mo. 10.

(442.) Izri Pool—another son of Martha Carver and William Pool, her husband—was born 1803, 9th month 29; married Evelina Terry in 1836, died 1859, 6th month 25. Had children:

1266. William Pool.
1267. Rachel Margaret Pool.
1268. Catharine Pool.
1269. Elizabeth Pool.
1270. Martha Pool.

(Martha[5], William[4], Joseph[3], William[2], William[1].)
(443.) Edward Q. Pool[6]—another son of Martha Carver and William Pool, her husband—was born 1809, 5th month 1; married Mary Thornton, 1840, 12th month 9, and resided in Lower Makefield Twp, Pa. Had children:

1271. Margaret Pool, b. 1842, 7 mo. 13, d. 1872, 1 mo. 15.
1272. Rachel Pool.
1273. Almira Pool.
1274. Martha Pool.
1275. Winfield S. Pool.

(Martha[5], William[4], Joseph[3], William[2], William[1].)
(444.) Thomas Pool[6]—another son of Martha Carver and William Pool, her husband—was born 1811, 2nd month 5, and died 1839, 8th month 24, not married.

(Martha[5], William[4], Joseph[3], William[2], William[1].)
(445.) Martha Pool[6]—another daughter of Martha Carver and William Pool, her husband—was born 1815, 12th month 18; married Samuel King and died 1875, 4th month 18, leaving one child:

1276. Thomas Clark King.

(446.) Catharine Streeper—a daughter of Elizabeth Carver and William Streeper, her husband—died unmarried.

(447.) Margaret Streeper—another daughter of Elizabeth Carver and William Streeper, her husband—died unmarried.

(Elizabeth[5], William[4], Joseph[3], William[2], William[1].)

(448.) Martha A. Streeper[6]—another daughter of Elizabeth Carver and William Streeper, her husband—married Isaac B. Terry. Had children:

1277. Elizabeth Terry.
1278. Margaret Terry.
1279. Franklin Terry.
1280. Miles Terry.
1281. Thomas Terry.
1282. Alma Terry.

(Elizabeth[5], William[4], Joseph[3], William[2], William[1].)

(449.) Elizabeth Streeper[6]—another daughter of Elizabeth Carver and William Streeper, her husband—married, first, John Hogeland, but had no children by him. Her second husband was Laurance Huber. They had but one child:

1283. William Huber.

(Hannah[5], William[4], Joseph[3], William[2], William[1].)

(450.) John Kimble, Jr.[6]—a son of Hannah Carver and John Kimble, her husband—was born in Buckingham in 1816, and was twice married: first, he was married, in 1841, to Catharine King, by whom he had his children; secondly, to Mary Stewart, 1876, 3d month 1. His children are:

1284. Caroline Kimble, b. in 1844.
1285. Enos Kimble, b. 1847, 7 mo. 31.
1286. William Kimble, b. 1849, 1 mo. 1.
1287. Lewis Kimble, b. 1856, 12 mo. 15, no children.
1288. Rosella Kimble, b. 1858, 8 mo. 5.
1289. Walter Kimble, b. 1860, 8 mo. 6.
1290. Mary Kimble, b. 1866, 11 mo. 28.
1291. Evan Kimble, b. 1869, 4 mo. 5.

(Hannah[5], William[4], Joseph[3], William[2], William[1].)

(451.) Martha Kimble[6]—a daughter of Hannah Carver and John Kimble, her husband—was born in Buckingham in 1812; married John McClure Bodine, son of David. Had children:

1292. Hannah Bodine.
1293. David Bodine.
1294. Martha Bodine, d. unm.
1295. Elizabeth Bodine, unm.
1296. Ella Bodine.
1297. Anna Bodine, d. at about 15 mo. old.

WILLIAM CARVER

(Hannah[5], William[4], Joseph[3], William[2], William[1].)

(452.) Hannah Kimble[6]—another daughter of Hannah Carver and John Kimble, her husband—was born in Buckingham, 1814, and married John Large of Buckingham. They now reside in the City of Philadelphia. Has children:

1298. William Large.
1299. Louisa Large.
1300. Elizabeth Large.
1301. Mary Ann Large.

(Hannah[5], William[4], Joseph[3], William[2], William[1].)

(453.) Elizabeth Kimble[6]—another daughter of Hannah Carver and John Kimble, her husband—was born in 1819; married Moses Blackson. Had children:

1302. John Blackson.
1303. Hannah Blackson, unm.

(Hannah[5], William[4], Joseph[3], William[2], William[1].)

(454.) George Washington Kimble[6]—another son of Hannah Carver and John Kimble, her husband—was born 1829; married Elizabeth Hoffman. Has one child:

1304. Oscar Kimble, m. and d. without children.

(Hannah[5], William[4], Joseph[3], William[2], William[1].)

(455.) Henry H. Kimble[6]—another son of Hannah Carver and John Kimble, her husband—was born in 1824; married Mary Titus, daughter of Seruch of Buckingham. Have children:

1305. Seruch Titus Kimble, b. 1849, 4 mo. 4.
1306. John Kimble.

(Izri[5], William[4], Joseph[3], William[2], Wiliam[1].)

(456.) William Carver[6]—a son of Izri Carver and Mary Hartley, his wife—married Eliza ———, and died leaving one child:

1307. Charles P. Carver, d. at about 2 years.

(457.) Martha P. Carver—a daughter of Izri Carver and Mary Hartley, his wife—married Jesse Ruth of Buckingham. Had children:

1308. William Ruth, d. unm.
1309. Helen Ruth, d. unm.
1310. Josephine Ruth, d. unm.
1311. Ivan Ruth, d. unm.
1312. Adam Ruth, d. unm.
1313. Edgar Ruth.
1314. George Ruth.
1315. Sallie Ruth.

GENEALOGY OF

(Izri[5], William[4], Joseph[3], William[2], William[1].)

(458.) Elizabeth H. Carver[6]—another daughter Izri Carver and Mary Hartley, his wife—married George Cook of New Hope, Pa. No children.

(459.) Rebecca Gillingham Elton—of Rachel Oldden and Thomas Elton, her husband—was born 1818, 6th month 25, died 1818, 9th month 21.

(Rachel[5], Elizabeth[4], Henry[3], William[2], William.[1])

(460.) Elizabeth Catharine Elton[6]—a daughter of Rachel Oldden and Thomas Elton, her husband—was born 1820, 3d month 2; and married Elias Livezey, son of Robert of Solebury Twp, Pa., and lives in Baltimore, Md. They had children:

1316. Francis Buck Livezey, b. 1845, 5 mo. 16.
1317. Thomas Elton Livezey, b. 1847, 2 mo. 4, d. 1847, 5 mo. 8.
1318. Paxton Elton Livezey, b. 1849, 12 mo. 28, d. 1855, 4 mo. 14.
1319. George Gillingham Livezey, b. 1856, 3 mo. 10, d. 1863, 3 mo. 12.
1320. Elizabeth Elton Livezey, b. 1858, 4 mo. 12.
1321. Josephine Livezey, b. 1861, 3 mo. 8.

(Rachel[5], Elizabeth[4], Henry[3], William[2], William[1].)

(461.) Josephine Gillingham Elton[6]—another daughter of Rachel Oldden and Thomas Elton, her husband—was born 1827, 3d month 27, and died 1850, 3d month 13.

(Hugh B.[5], Rachel[4], Henry[3], William[2], William[1].)

(462.) Achsah M. Ely[6]—a daughter of Hugh B. Ely and Sarah Oldden, his wife—was born 1815, 9th month 25; married Joseph Holmes Davis of New Jersey, and died leaving one child:

1322. Mary Oldden Davis.

(Hugh B.[5], Rachel[4], Henry[3], William[2], William[1].)

(463.) Mary Anna Ely[6]—another daughter of Hugh B. Ely and Sarah Oldden, his wife—was born in Buckingham, 1816, 11th month 20; married Moses Eastburn of Solebury, 1845, 3d month, and died in 1873. Had children:

1323. Hugh B. Eastburn, b. 1846, 2 mo. 11.
1324. Fanney C. Eastburn, b. 1847, 10 mo. 27, d. young.

(Hugh B.[5], Rachel[4], Henry[3], William[2], William[1].)

(464.) Francenia Ely[6]—another daughter of Hugh B. Ely and Sarah Oldden, his wife—was born in Buckingham, 1818, 1st month 26; married John Blackfan of Solebury, and died 1895, 4th month 26, at Yardley. No children.

WILLIAM CARVER

(Hugh B.[5], Rachel[4], Henry[3], William[2], William[1].)

(465.) Joseph Oldden Ely[6]—a son of Hugh B. Ely and Sarah Oldden, his wife—was born in Buckingham, 1820, 2nd month 10. Had one child:

1325. Alfred E. Ely.

(466.) Alfred Ely—another son of Hugh B. Ely and Sarah Oldden, his wife—was born 1822, 9th month 25; died young.

(Hugh B.[5], Rachel[4], Henry[3], William[2], William[1].)

(467.) Charles Bennington Ely[6]—another son of Hugh B. Ely and Sarah Oldden, his wife—was born in Buckingham, 1824, 9th month 1; married Mary Kirk of Buckingham. Had children:

1326. Jane K. Ely.
1327. Hugh B. Ely.
1328. William Penn Ely.
1329. Walter Ely.
1330. Lettie Ely.

(Hugh B.[5], Rachel[4], Henry[3], William[2], William[1].)

(468.) William Penn Ely[6]—another son of Hugh B. Ely and Sarah Oldden, his wife—was born in Solebury, 1827, 2nd month 6; married Phebe Baker and died in 1856. He had one child:

1331. *Sarah Ely.

(William C.[5], Rachel[4], Henry[3], William[2], William[1].)

(469.) Catharine O. Ely[6]—a daughter of William C. Ely and Lydia D. Hulse, his wife—was born 1836, 5th month 5, died 1853, 4th month 30.

(470.) Hugh B. Ely—a son of William C. Ely and Lydia D. Hulse, his wife—was born 1838, 3d month 9; married Theresa J. Herbert, 1868, 7th month 8; she was born 1839, 5th month 20. They had children:

1332. Catharine H. Ely, b. 1869, 5 mo. 30.
1333. Rachel Ely, b. 1870, 6 mo. 29.
1334. Mary D. Ely, b. 1873, 2 mo. 1.
1335. Hugh B. Ely, b. 1875, 11 mo. 5.
1336. Grace Holmes Ely, b. 1880, 3 mo. 25, d. 1880, 4 mo. 10.

(William C.⁵, Rachel⁴, Henry³, William², William¹.)

(471.) Rachel S. Ely⁶—a daughter of William C. Ely and Lydia D. Hulse, his wife—was born 1840, 6th month 29; married Joseph Romine, 1861, 10th month 23. They live at present at Rochester, Mich. Have children:

1337. Hugh B. Romine, b. 1864, 6 mo. 13.
1338. Jessie E. Romine, b. 1866, 3 mo. 23.
1339. Lydia D. E. Romine, d. 1868, 3 mo. 4.
1340. Joseph E. Romine, b. 1869, 10 mo. 19.
1341. Nellie H. Romine, b. 1871, 6 mo. 7.
1342. Ruth Hull Romine, 1873, 4 mo. 9.
1343. William C. Ely Romine, b. 1875, 2 mo. 6.
1343¼. Cora Kate Romine, b. 1877, 4 mo. 21.
1343½. Carrie Beegle Romine, b. 1879, 12 mo. 27.
1344. Robert Talpot Romine.

(William C.⁵, Rachel⁴, Henry³, William², William¹.)

(472.) Elizabeth Carver Ely⁶—another daughter of William C. Ely and Lydia D. Hulse, his wife—was born 1842, 10th month 13; married, 1863, 6th month 27, at Stockton, N. J., Silas Huffman La Rue. Have children:

1345. Holmes Ely La Rue, b. at West Chester, Pa., 1865, 7 mo. 1.
1346. John Guyot La Rue, b. at Lewisburg, Pa., 1867, 7 mo. 12.
1347. Theodore Bega La Rue, b. at Allentown, Pa., 1869, 7 mo. 11.
1348. Martha Schofield La Rue, b. at Allentown, Pa., 1871, 11 mo. 16.
1349. Silas Palissy La Rue, b, at Frenchtown, N. J., 1874, 2 mo. 21.
1350. Elizabeth Ely La Rue, b. at Frenchtown, N. J., 1878, 12 mo. 22.
1351. Warran Jacques La Rue, b. at Reading, Pa., 1881, 10 mo. 29, d. 1883, 3 mo. 31.
1352. James Malcom La Rue, b. at Reading, Pa., 1883, 12 mo. 6.

(William C.⁵, Rachel⁴, Henry³, William², William¹.)

(473.) Holmes D. Ely⁶—another son of William C. Ely and Lydia D. Hulse, his wife—was born 1845, 3d month 11; married Matilda ———, 1868, 3d month 18. She was born in 1844, 7th month 11. They reside at Lambertville, N. J. Have children:

1353. Lilian Stead Ely, b. 1869, 4 mo. 4.
1354. William Parker Ely, b. 1870, 12 mo. 7.
1355. John Anderson Ely, b. 1872, 5 mo. 4.
1356. Alfred Thomas Ely, b. 1873, 10 mo. 24.
1357. Mary Anna Eastburn Ely, b. 1875, 5 mo. 25.
1358. Holmes Davis Ely, b. 1877, 11 mo. 9, d. 1878, 1 mo. 26.

(474.) Richard Watson Ely[6]—another son of William C. Ely and Lydia D. Hulse, his wife—was born 1847, 3d month 6, died 1848, 1st month 16.

(William C.[5], Rachel[4], Henry[3] William[2], William[1].)
(475.) Sarah Y. Ely[6]—another daughter of William C. Ely and Lydia D. Hulse, his wife—was born 1849, 4th month 22. Not married.

(476.) Thomas H. Ely[6]—another son of William C. Ely and Lydia D. Hulse, his wife—born 1851, 10th month 16, died 1855, 7th month 13.

(477.) William C. Ely, Jr.[6]—another son of William C. Ely and Lydia D. Hulse, his wife—was born 1854, 9th month 30, died 1875, 4th month 7.

(David[5], Thomas[4], Henry[3], William[2], William[1].)
(478.) Elizabeth W. Carver[6]—a daughter of David Carver and Ann Walker, his wife—was born in Solebury, Pa., 1817, 9th month 26; married Jesse Black, son of Abraham. She died about 1853 or 1854, leaving children:

1359. Jonathan W. Black.
1360. Lorenzo D. Black.
1361. Edwin Black.

(David[5], Thomas[4], Henry[3], William[2], William[1].)
(479.) Asenath Carver[6]—another daughter of David Carver and Ann Walker, his wife—was born in Solebury, Pa., 1819, 12th month 19; married Alfred H. Barber, and died in the Borough of Doylestown, on Sunday, July 19th, 1895, æt. 65 years, 7 months. Her children are:

1362. Elizabeth W. Barber.
1363. Elliston P. Barber.
1363½. Mary Arrilla Barber.
1364. Amos Walker Barber, M.D.
1365. Meta Bell Barber.

(David[5], Thomas[4], Henry[3], William[2], William[1].)
(480.) Sarah Ann Carver[6]—another daughter of David Carver and Ann Walker, his wife—was born in Solebury, Pa., 1829, 10th month 25; married Charles Flack, who died in Buckingham in 1875. Has children:

1366. Howard W. Flack, b. 1860, 7 mo. 5.
1367. John Dyer Flack, b. 1864, 4 mo. 30.

(Pamelia[5], John[4], Henry[3], William[2], William[1].)
(481.) Ann Eliza Wanamaker[6]—a daughter of Pamelia Carver and Nicholas Wanamaker, her husband—was born 1812, 8th month 16; married William S. Barron, 1856, 9th month 25. She died at Centrebridge, Bucks Co., Pa., on Monday, 1884, 7th month 7, æt. 71 years, 6 months, 20 days. Had no children.

(Pamelia[5], John[4], Henry[3], William[2], William[1].)

(482.) Letitia Wanamaker[6]—another daughter of Pamelia Carver and Nicholas Wanamaker, her husband—was born 1817, 2nd month 23; married William Robinson, 1836, 2nd month 4. Her children are:

1368. Ann Rebecca Robinson, b. 1836, 11 mo. 2.
1369. D. Clinton Robinson, b. 1846, 1 mo. 22, d. unm.
1370. William H. Robinson, b. 1849, 12 mo. 23.

(483.) Mary G. Wanamaker—a daughter of Pamelia Carver and Nicholas Wanamaker, her husband—was born 1819, 3d month 5; married Samuel Cowgill, son of Thomas of Plumstead, 1861, 3d month 14. She died at Centrebridge, Bucks Co., Pa., 1885, 4th month 27, æt. 66 years, 1 month, 22 days. They had no children.

(484.) Thomas C. Wanamaker—a son of Nicholas Wanamaker and Pamelia Carver, his wife—was born 1824, 8th month 10; married Hannah Ann Romine. No children.

(485.) John E. Wanamaker—another son of Pamelia Carver and Nicholas Wanamaker, her husband—was born 1826, 7th month 6, died, unmarried, 1844, 10th month 11.

(486.) Anna U. Wanamaker—another daughter of Pamelia Carver and Nicholas Wanamaker, her husband—was born 1830, 1st month 4; married Thomas B. Scott, 1854, 3d month 9. Have children:

1371. Winfield Scott, b. 1854, 12 mo. 15, d. 1855, 8 mo. 3.
1372. Victoria R. Scott, b. 1856, 7 mo. 9, d. 1857, 2 mo. 18.
1373. Anna Pamelia Scott, b. 1858, 4 mo. 7, d. 1860, 10 mo. 6.
1374. Thomas B. Scott, Jr., b. 1860, 7 mo. 14, d. 1860, 9 mo. 10.
1375. Joseph N. Scott, b. 1861, 8 mo. 31.
1376. Bella R. Scott, b. 1863, 6 mo. 30.

(Pamelia[5], John[4], Henry[3], William[2], William[1].)

(487.) Alfred Wanamaker[6]—another son of Pamelia Carver and Nicholas Wanamaker, her husband—was born 1832, 1st month 11; married Melissa Webster, 1857, 6th month 25. Had children:

1377. Edward Wanamaker, b. 1860, 6 mo. 12.
1378. Charlotte W. Wanamaker, b. 1868, 10 mo. 2.
1379. Jennie Wanamaker, b. 1877, 5 mo. 25.

WILLIAM CARVER

(Pamelia[5], John[4], Henry[3], William[2], William[1].)

(488.) Henry C. Wanamaker[6]—another son of Pamelia Carver and Nicholas Wanamaker, her husband—was twice married: first, to Rachel Hendricks in 1860, 2nd month 28, by whom he had children. She died and he married, secondly, 1878, 9th month 21, Ellen L. Moore. His children are:

1380. Elizabeth C. Wanamaker, b. 1861, 11 mo. 30.
1381. Mary C. Wanamaker, b. 1864, 5 mo. 15.
1382. Jennie S. Wanamaker, b. 1867, 6 mo. 28, d. 1867, 9 mo. 27.
1383. Sadie F. Wanamaker, b. 1868, 12 mo. 7.

(Sarah Ann[5], John[4], Henry[3], William[2], William[1].)

(489.) Alfred Shaw, Esq.[6]—a son of Sarah Ann Carver and Joseph Prior Shaw, her husband—was born in Bucks Co., Pa., 1830, went to New Orleans when quite a young man, taught school there, and became superintendent of the schools; studied law in that city and was engaged in the practice of it at the time of the Rebellion. He came North during the war and was suspected of being a spy, and some effort was made to arrest him. But he was true to his country and his country's flag. He died in New Orleans, suddenly, on Monday evening, 1886, 11th month 15, of apoplexy. He spoke, in addition to the English language, Spanish and French. He married Martha Johnson, daughter of William H. Johnson of Buckingham, Bucks Co., Pa., in 1856. Had children:

1384. Mary J. Shaw, b. 1858.
1385. Alfred Shaw, Jr., b. 1861, d. in 1872.

(490.) Anna Shaw—a daughter of Sarah Ann Carver and Joseph Prior Shaw, her husband—was born in 1830, died in 1837.

(Sarah Ann[5], John[4], Henry[3], William[2], William[1].)

(491.) Marietta Shaw[6]—another daughter of Sarah Ann Carver and Joseph Prior Shaw, her husband—was born 1834; married Edward Seiter Barber in 1853, died in 1858, leaving one child:

1386. Edward Shaw Barber, b. 1856.

(Sarah Ann[5], John[4], Henry[3], William[2], William[1].)

(492.) John Wilson Shaw[6]—another son of Sarah Ann Carver and Joseph Prior Shaw, her husband—was born in 1837; married Diana Wornark in 1862, and died in 1870, leaving one child:

1387. Ettie Prior Shaw, b. in 1864.

(Letitia[5], John[4], Henry[3], William[2], William[1].)

(493.) J. Watson Case[6]—a son of Letitia Ellicott Carver and Alexander Johnson Case, her husband—was born 1826, 11th month 24; married Maria P. Scarborough, 1852, 2nd month 19, and died in Doylestown Boro, 1886, 5th month 10. Had children:

1388. Harriet S. Case, b. 1852, 11 mo. 21.
1389. Letitia C. Case, b. 1855, 11 mo. 18.
1390. Sarah E. Case, b. 1857, 10 mo. 5, d. 1858, 4 mo. 1.
1391. Edward G. Case, b. 1860, 3 mo. 31.
1392. Martha E. Case, b. 1862, 5 mo. 31.

(494.) Sarah A. Case—a daughter of Letitia Ellicott Carver and Alexander Johnson Case, her husband—was born in Buckingham, 1828, 8th month 30; married Samuel Carey Longshore, 1852, 2nd month 12, and died in 1856, 11th month 21; no children.

(Letitia[5], John[4], Henry[3], William[2], William[1].)

(495.) William E. Case, M.D.[6]—another son of Letitia Ellicott Carver and Alexander Johnson Case, her husband—was born in Buckingham, 1831, 1st month 2, and was twice married: first, to Martha Price, by whom he had two children; secondly, to Roxanna Parsons—had one child by her. He studied medicine, and is practicing in Trenton. N. J. Has children:

1393. William Schuyler Case, b. 1862, 6 mo. 6.
1394. Philip A. Case, b. 1866, 4 mo. 4.
1395. Anna Parsons Case, b. 1879, 9 mo. 28.

(Letitia[5], John[4], Henry[3], William[2], William[1].)

(496.) Caroline B. Case[6]—another daughter of Letitia Ellicott Carver and Alexander Johnson Case, her husband—was born 1833, 2nd month 14; married Daniel Wharton, 1861, 4th month 4. Has one child:

1396. Rebecca Case Wharton, b. 1867, 10 mo. 2.

(Letitia[5], John[4], Henry[3], William[2], William[1].)

(497.) Henry C. Case[6]—another son of Letitia Ellicott Carver and Alexander Johnson Case, her husband—was born 1835, 8th month 9; married Sarah Sands, 1857, 4th month 9. Has children:

1397. Mary W. Case, b. 1858, 5 mo. 3.
1398. Caroline S. Case, b. 1861, 8 mo. 16, d. 1864, 5 mo. 19.
1399. Florence N. Case, b. 1869, 9 mo. 21.
1400. Samuel S. Case, b. 1871, 6 mo. 21.
1401. Horace E. Case, b. 1875, 9 mo. 12.

WILLIAM CARVER

(Letitia[5], John[4], Henry[3], William[2], William[1].)

(498.) Rebecca C. Case[6]—another daughter of Letitia Ellicott Case and Alexander Johnson Case, her husband—was born 1839, 10th month 9; married Edward Helwig, son of Daniel, 1867, 11th month 20. She has one child:

1402. Frank Helwig, b. 1871, 12 mo. 9, d. next day.

(499.) Elizabeth F. Case—another daughter of Letitia Elicott Case and Alexander Johnson Case, her husband—was born 1836, 12th month 13, died 1836, 10th month 16.

(Letitia[5], John[4], Henry[3], William[2], William[1].)

(500.) Samuel C. Case[6]—another son of Letitia Ellicott Case and Alexander Johnson Case, her husband—was born 1843, 8th month 2; married Anna E. Slack, 1869, 12 mo. 2. Have children:

1403. Nettie DuBoise Case, b. 1870, 10 mo. 26.
1404. Henry Carver Case, b. 1874, 12 mo. 22.
1405. Ella Black Case, b. 1876, 3 mo. 9, d. 1876, 9 mo. 2.

(John[5], John[4], Henry[3], William[2], William[1].)

(501.) Thomas J. Carver[6]—a son of John Ellicott Carver and Eliza Grim Nicholson, his wife—was born in Philadelphia in 1838; married Caroline E. Douglas, and died in Philadelphia, 1863, 7th month 3, leaving one child, now living in Wilmington, Del.:

1406. John Douglas Carver, b. 1859, 4 mo.

(John[5], John[4], Henry[3], William[2], William[1].)

(502.) William Henry Harrison Carver[6]—another son of John Ellicott Carver and Eliza Grim Nicholson, his wife—was born in the City of Philadelphia, 1841, 3d month 14; married Mary Wareham Ross, 1877, 5th month 16. He is a conveyancer and has one child:

1407. Ellicott Carver, b. 1882, 11 mo 26.

(503.) Ann Rebecca Carver—daughter of John Carver and Sarah Ellicott, his wife—was born 1842, 4th month 12, died 1864, 6th month 13, not married.

(Henry[5], John[4], Henry[3], William[2], William[1].)

(504.) Sarah Grace Carver[6]—a daughter of Henry Ellicott Carver and Elizabeth Shaw, his wife—died 1857, 10th month 3, not married.

(Thomas[5], Joseph[4], Henry[3], William[2], William[1].)

(505.) Joseph Carver[6]—a son of Thomas Carver and Tamson Gray, his wife—was born in Harrisville, Ohio, 1818, 11th month 7; married Sarah Bashore, 1842, 1st month 22, and died in 1845, 5th month 5, leaving a widow and one child:

1408. Maria Louisa Carver, b. 1844, 2 mo. 18, d. 1846.

(Thomas[5], Joseph[4], Henry[3], William[2], William[1].)

(506.) Elizabeth Ann Carver[6]—a daughter of Thomas Carver of Harrisville, Ohio, and Tamson Gray, his wife—was born in Harrisville, Ohio, 1821, 4th month 29, and married Jeremiah Booth, 1838, 9th month 23. They live near Arlington, Bureau Co., Ill. Have children:

1409. Joseph Carver Booth, b. 1840, 1 mo. 21.
1410. Julia Arabella Booth, b. 1842, 8 mo. 23.
1411. Mary Elizabeth Booth, b. 1844, 10 mo. 11, d. 1866, 8 mo. 23.
1412. William Hoyle Booth, b. 1847, 10 mo. 21.
1413. Emily Jane Booth, b. 1850, 5 mo. 8.

(Thomas[5], Joseph[4], Henry[3], William[2], William[1].)

(507.) Hannah Carver[6]—another daughter of Thomas Carver and Tamson Gray, his wife—was born at Harrisville, Ohio, 1824, 4th month 6, d. 1833, 7th month 5.

(Thomas[5], Joseph[4], Henry[3], William[2], William[1].)

(508.) Julia Ann Carver[6]—another daughter of Thomas Carver and Tamson Gray, his wife—was born at Harrisville, Ohio, 1830, 11th month 14; was twice married: first, to Lewas W. Watson (who was born 1827, 2nd month 2), 1846, 2nd month 16; they had five children. He died in 1861, 5th month 25. Secondly, she married Ephramin Kibble (who was born 1833, 2nd month 16) in 1863, 3d month 16. They had two children, to wit:

1414. William H. Watson, b. 1848, 6 mo. 29, d. 1849, 7 mo. 13.
1415. Albert C. Watson, b. 1849, 7 mo. 30, d. 1849, 12 mo. 28.
1416. Thomas Wesley Watson, b. 1850, 9 mo. 21.
1417. Emma Florence Watson, b. 1853, 7 mo. 11.
1418. Narcissa Watson, b. 1856, 3 mo. 26.
1419. William H. Kibble, b. 1865, 1 mo. 8.
1420. Adda Gray Kibble, b. 1872, 10 mo. 10.

(Thomas[5], Joseph[4], Henry[3], William[2], William[1].)

(509.) Mary J. Carver[6]—another daughter of Thomas Carver and Tamson Gray, his wife—was born in Harrisville, Ohio, 1827, 2nd month 7; married Thomas Nicholson, 1847, 6th month 8. Her children are:

1421. Julia Ann Nicholson, b. 1848, 8 mo. 21.
1422. William Addison Nicholson, b. 1850, 3 mo. 17.
1423. Mary Emma Nicholson, b. 1852, 7 mo. 22.
1424. Eva Virginia Nicholson, b. 1855, 2 mo. 18.
1425. Elizabeth B. Nicholson, b. 1859, 8 mo. 8, } twins; d. same day.
1426. Sarah Jane Nicholson, b. 1859, 8 mo. 8,

(Thomas[5], Joseph[4], Henry[3], William[2], William[1].)

(510.) Emily Carver[6]—another daughter of Thomas Carver and Tamson Gray, his wife—was born in Harrisville, Ohio, 1835, 6th month 14; married William H. Roach, 1852, 1st month 22. Had children:

1427. Thomas Carver Roach, b. 1853, 1 mo. 1.
1428. James Franklin Roach, b. 1853, 7 mo. 13, d. 1858, 5 mo. 12.
1429. Ella Lucinda Roach, b. 1857, 4 mo. 16.
1430. William Harvey Roach, b. 1859, 4 mo. 5.
1431. Joseph Booth Roach, b. 1861, 2 mo. 17.
1432. Albert Clifton Roach, b. 1863, 2 mo. 27.
1433. Frederick Sherman Roach, b. 1865, 2 mo. 2.
1434. Clarence Franklin Roach, b. 1867, 2 mo. 28, d. 1867, 9 mo. 21.
1435. Clara Tamson Roach, b. 1869, 2 mo. 22.
1436. George Fogle Roach, b. 1871, 9 mo. 21.
1437. Eva Virginia Roach, b. 1874, 1 mo. 13.

(Henry[5], Joseph[4], Henry[3], William[2], William[1].)

(511.) Elizabeth B. Carver[6]—a daughter of Henry Carver and Hannah Paxson, his wife—was born in Carversville, Solebury Twp, Bucks Co., Pa., 1816, 2nd month 17. She was married at Trenton, N. J., before the Mayor, on 5th day, 1854, 10th month 12, to Joseph C. Slack of Northampton Twp, Bucks Co., Pa., who was born 1826, 1st month 1. He died at the Belmont Hotel, in Fulton Street, New York, on Sunday night, 1881, 8th month 21, where he had stopped on his return from Ocean Grove, aged 55 years, 7 months, 21 days. Elizabeth B., his wife, died in Northampton Twp, Bucks Co., Pa., where they lived, Wednesday, 1887, 5th month 18, at 20 minutes before 5 o'clock, afternoon, æt. 71 years, 3 months, 1 day. They had but one child living:

1438. Henrietta C. Slack, b. 5th day, 1858, 4 mo. 8.

(Henry⁵, Joseph⁴, Henry³, William², William¹.)

(512.) Elias Carver⁶—a son of Henry Carver and Hannah Paxson, his wife—was born in Carversville, Solebury Twp, Bucks Co., Pa., 1817, 10th month 12. He studied law with the Hon. Stokes L. Roberts, in the Boro of Doylestown, Pa., and was admitted to the Bar of Bucks Co., Pa., April 30, 1845. He practiced law there and was elected District Attorney in the fall of 1850, and was installed into office and took his seat as District Attorney, the first Monday of December 1845, being the first District Attorney elected in Bucks Co. The term was for three years.

He and Rebecca McIntosh, daughter of John and Hannah Hughes, his wife, were married on 5th day of the week, 1860, 2nd month 23. She died suddenly on 7th day afternoon, 1874, 10th month 17, about quarter before 5 o'clock. They had one child:

1439. Henry Carver, b. on 4th day, 1860, 12 mo. 12, in Doylestown Boro, about 30 minutes past 3 o'clock, P.M.

He is a graduate of Yale University of Class 1883, and also of the Law Department of the University of Pennsylvania of Class 1886. He practices law in the City of Philadelphia.

(513.) A son was born of Rachel Carver and Joseph Broadhurst, her husband, 1817, 3d month 26, and died the same day.

(Rachel⁵, Joseph⁴, Henry³, William², William¹.)

(514.) Mary Anna Broadhurst⁶—a daughter of Rachel Carver and Joseph Broadhurst, her husband—was born 1818, 9th month 16. She and Samuel Johnson Paxson were married at Buckingham Monthly Meeting of Friends, 1840, 4th month 15. He published for many years, in the Borough of Doylestown, a weekly paper called *The Doylestown Democrat*, and died in Buckingham, 1864, 5th month 28, æt. 46 years, 5 months, 7 days. They had several children who died young; only two survived:

1440. Helen M. Paxson, m. J. Hart Bye.
1441. Carrie R. Paxson, m. Watson Malone.

(Rachel⁵, Joseph⁴, Henry³, William², William¹.)

(515.) Samuel E. Broadhurst⁶—a son of Rachel Carver and Joseph Broadhurst, her husband—was born in Philadelphia, 1823, 2d month 25; married 1848, 2d month 3, Sarah J. Reeder, a daughter of Sarah Twining and Charles Reeder, her husband, and grand-daughter of Elias Reeder. She died 1874, 4th month 23. They had children:

1442. Joseph J. Broadhurst, a lawyer.
1443. Anna M. Broadhurst, d. 1872, 8 mo. 9.
1444. Horace Greely Broadhurst.

(Rachel[5], Joseph[4], Henry[3], William[2], William[1].)

(516.) Caroline L. Broadhurst[6]—another daughter of Rachel Carver and Joseph Broadhurst, her husband—was born 1826, 10th month 17. She and Oliver Howard Wilson were married 1846, 1st month 15. They live in the City of Philadelphia, and have two children:

1445. Julius Wilson.
1446. Caroline Wilson.

(Mary[5], Joseph[4], Henry[3], William[2], William[1].)

(517.) Charles Eastburn[6]—a son of Mary Carver and Samuel Eastburn, her husband—was born in Solebury Twp, Bucks Co., Pa., 1825, 5th month 24. He traveled a good deal over the Western States on foot, visiting General Cass' residence in Michigan and Henry Clay's in Kentucky. When the War of the Rebellion broke forth in 1861, he enlisted at Dubuque as a private in Company B, 9th Regiment of Iowa Volunteers, September 2nd, 1861, William Vandevere commanding; but at the time of his death, Carokaddon, Colonel, commanded. His captain was Paul Sweeney. The regiment was under U. S. Grant, and at the Siege of Vicksburg, Charles was struck with a fragment of a shell on July 3d, 1863, and died that evening, unmarrried. Vicksburg surrendered July 4th, 1863. He was praised by his captain as being a good soldier.

(Mary[5], Joseph[4], Henry[3], William[2], William[1].)

(518.) Henry C. Eastburn[6]—another son of Mary Carver and Samuel Eastburn, her husband—was born in Solebury Twp, Pa., 1827, 2d month 17; went to California over land; not caring to remain there he went to Dallas, Polk Co., Oregon, and remained there seven years. He returned to Bucks Co. with several thousand dollars in gold. Subsequently he went to Texas and died there in 1878, 10th month 12; unmarried.

(519.) Joseph C. Eastburn—another son of Mary Carver and Samuel Eastburn, her husband—was born in Solebury, Pa., 1829, 2d month 3, died 1830, 3d month 5.

(Mary[5], Joseph[4], Henry[3], William[2], William[1].)

(520.) Edward Eastburn[6]—another son of Mary Carver and Samuel Eastburn her husband—was born in Solebury, Pa., in 1831, 1st month 9; went before he was 21 years old to New Orleans. There he became acquainted with a young Scotchman who was a tanner and currier. They walked from there to the southern part of Alabama where they bought one acre of land for about $2.50, taking nearly all their money. They went to work like northern men, sinking vats, asking people to trust them till they got leather tanned and sold, and they would then pay all their debts. They were trusted. In a short time they had quite a tan yard, paid their debts, bought other land, built tenant houses on it for tenants, got shoemakers to make the leather up and became quite well off when the War of the Rebellion was threatening. They then closed up their business and separated. Edward was forced into the Rebel Army, made his escape; went into Arkansas where he was pursued as a deserter, but was not caught. He went into Mexico, bought a large quantity of cotton and hauled it to the City of Mexico and sold it there. He bought large droves of cattle and sold them in Kansas. He finally settled in Jacksboro, Jack Co., Texas. He became wealthy, worth over a half a million of dollars. He traveled a great deal over the United States and in Europe, and died in the City of Philadelphia, Pa., August 20, 1900, when on a visit.

(521.) Hannah Eastburn—a daughter of Mary Carver and Samuel Eastburn, her husband—was born 1833, 6th month 13; married Anthony Worthington of Buckingham, 1854, 4th month 25, and died in California, Saturday, January 7th, 1888, æt, 54 years, 6 months, 24 days. Had children:

1447. Edwin R. Worthington, b. 1856, 2 mo. 5.
1448. Samuel E. Worthington, b. 1858, 4 mo. 24, d. in Kansas 1878, 7 mo. 2.
1449. Linford E. Worthington, b. 1862, 8 mo. 19, d. in Kansas 1881, 1 mo.; he lived in California, leaving wife and one child:
1450. Warran Worthington, b. 1864, 7 mo. 13.

(522.) Rachel Eastburn—another daughter of Mary Carver and Samuel Eastburn, her husband—was born in Buckingham Twp, Pa., 1835, 9th month 13, died 1836, 9th month 13.

(523.) Rachel Smith—a daughter of Anne Carver and Samuel Smith, her husband—was born in Solebury Twp, Bucks Co., Pa., 1837, 12th month. Not married; died 1902.

(Eli[5], Joseph[4], Henry[3], William[2], William[1].)

(524.) Mary Anna B. Carver[6]—a daughter of Eli Carver and Martha P. Ross, his wife—was born in Solebury Twp, 1833, 8th month 2; married in 1856, Curtis Missimer of Philadelphia, and died in Northampton Twp, Bucks Co., Pa., near Sackett's Ford, 1880, 11th month 9, leaving a daughter:

1451. Martha Carver Messimer.

(525.) Jenkens R. Carver—a son of Eli Carver and Martha P. Ross, his wife—was born 1835. Twin; know nothing.

(526.) Joseph C. Carver—a son of Eli Carver and Martha P. Ross, his wife—was born 1835. Twin; know nothing.

(527.) Elizabeth F. Carver—another daughter of Eli Carver and Martha P. Ross, his wife—was born in Solebury, 1837, 7th month 7; married 1859, 12th month 10, Washington F. Chrisman of Chester Co., Pa. No children.

(Eli[5], Joseph[4], Henry[3], William[2], William[1].)

(528.) Hannah C. Carver[6]—another daughter of Eli Carver and Martha P. Ross, his wife—was born in Solebury, 1838, 10th month; married, when in her 24th year, Dr. William Henry Daniels of Philadelphia. Have no children.

(529.) Charles R. Carver—another son of Eli Carver and Martha P. Ross, his wife—was born in Solebury; died about 10 years of age.

(Eli[5], Joseph[4], Henry[3], William[2], William[1].)

(530.) Cephes Ross Carver[6]—another son of Eli Carver and Martha P. Ross, his wife—was born in Solebury. Served in U. S. Army during the Rebellion; returned home and soon after married Emma J. Harp. Children:

1452. Henry E. Carver.
1453. William D. Carver, d. in infancy.
1454. Fannie H. Carver, d. 1882, 1 mo.
1455. William Carver.

(531.) Cecelia E. Carver—another daughter of Eli Carver and Martha P. Ross, his wife—married Albert Lineaweaver, son of Dr. Lineaweaver of Lebanon, Pa., she being in her 19th year. Has one child:

1456. Walter Lineaweaver.

(532.) Eli Carver, Jr.—another son of Eli Carver and Martha P. Ross, his wife—was born in Solebury; lived several years in France. Not married.

GENEALOGY OF

(533.) **Martha Emma Carver**—another daughter of Eli Carver and Martha P. Ross, his wife—married Oliver P. Walton when in her 18th year. Have one child:

1457. Arrita D. Walton.

(534.) **Eber Leamon Carver**—another son of Eli Carver and Martha P. Ross, his wife—married Hannah Fisher of Philadelphia. Have children:

1458. Fannie Carver.
1459. Milton Carver.
1460. Jennie Carver.
1461. ——— Carver.
1462. ——— Carver.

(Eli[5], Joseph[4], Henry[3], William[2], William[1].)

(535.) **Walter Scott Carver**[6]—another son of Eli Carver and Martha P. Ross, his wife—was born 1857, 2nd month 6; married 1881, 12th month 24, to ——— of New York City. Have one child:

1463. Emma C. Carver.

(Eli[5], Joseph[4], Henry[3], William[2], William[1].)

(536.) **Edward Paxson Carver**[6]—another son of Eli Carver and Martha P. Ross, his wife—entered the Navy of the United States prior to the War of the Rebellion and served during that period. Since then his whereabouts is unknown. Probably he may be dead. Not married:

(537.) **Oliver C. Allen**—a son of Julia H. Carver and Elihu W. Allen, her husband—was born 1831, 1st month 3, died 1836, 8th month 4, in Ohio.

(Julia[5], Joseph[4], Henry[3], William[2], William[1].)

(538.) **Alfred E. Allen**[6]—another son of Julia H. Carver and Elihu W. Allen, her husband—was born 1832, 12th month 30. He was twice married: first, to Mary Jane Closson, by whom he had his children; secondly, to Clara Clark. He died suddenly, being killed by machinery in 1883. His children are:

1464. Samuel Allen.
1465. William Allen.
1466. Harry Allen.

(Julia[5], Joseph[4], Henry[3], William[2], William[1].)

(539.) **Caroline W. Allen**[6]—a daughter of Julia H. Carver and Elihu W. Allen, her husband—was born 1834, 10th month 28, and was twice married: first, to John Wiley of Solebury, 1852, 2nd month 28. He died 1859, 4th month. Her second husband was Samuel Rose of Solebury, Bucks Co., Pa.; they were married 1860, 10th month 14. He died 1882, 9th month 1. Her children are:

WILLIAM CARVER

1467. George Wiley, b. 1856, 12 mo. 31.
1468. Anne Rose, by second husband.
1469. Lizzie Rose, by second husband.

(Julia⁵, Joseph⁴, Henry³, William², William¹.)

(540.) Joseph C. Allen⁶—another son of Julia H. Carver and Elihu W. Allen, her husband—was born 1837, 7th month 15; married; has children:

1470. Walter Allen.
1471. Howard Allen.
1472. William Allen.

(541.) Hannah A. Allen—another daughter of Julia H. Carver and Elihu W. Allen—was born in Solebury Twp, 1841, 4th month 17, died in 1844.

(542.) Mary B. Allen—another daughter of Julia H. Carver and Elihu W. Allen, her husband—was born in Solebury, 1843, 5th month 18; married Abel Tomlinson, and reside in New Jersey. No children.

(Julia⁵, Joseph⁴, Henry³, William², William¹.)

(543.) Martha C. Allen⁶—another daughter of Julia H. Carver and Elihu W. Allen, her husband—was born in Solebury, 1845, 12th month 6; married Allen Ely. Have children:

1473. Abel Ely.
1474. William Ely.
1475. Mary Ely.

(544.) Elizabeth C. Allen—another daughter of Julia H. Carver and Elihu W. Allen, her husband—was born in Solebury, 1848, 10th month 3, died 1850.

(Julia⁵, Joseph⁴, Henry³, William², William¹.)

(545.) Rachel S. Allen⁶—another daughter of Julia H. Carver and Elihu W. Allen, her husband—was born in Solebury Twp, 1852, 4th month 30; married William Hayes of Solebury. Have children:

1476. Mary Hayes.
1477. Charles Hayes.

(Amos⁵, Benjamin⁴, Henry³, William², William¹.)

(545½.) Rachel Carver⁶—a daughter of Amos Carver and Elizabeth Lewis, his wife—was born in Plumstead Twp, 1814, 10th month 20; married David Caffee, and died childless, 1878, 4th month 21.

(Amos⁵, Benjamin⁴, Henry³, William², William¹.)

(546.) Benjamin Carver⁶—a son of Amos Carver and Elizabeth Lewis, his wife—went to Canada.

(547.) Mordecai Carver—another son of Amos Carver and Elizabeth Lewis, his wife—was born in Blumstead Twp, 1818, 12th month 31; married 1841, 9th month 1, Cyrene Hellyer, daughter of David Hellyer. He died at the residence of his brother-in-law, William Lukens, 1884, 12th month 15, æt. 65 years, 11 months. No children.

(Amos[5], Benjamin[4], Henry[3], William[2], William[1].)

(548.) Sarah Carver[6]—another daughter of Amos Carver and Elizabeth Lewis, his wife—was born 1820, 9th month 23; married John G. Casner, 1836, 11th month 10. Had children:

1478. Benjamin Casner, b. 1837, 2 mo. 9.
1479. Samuel Casner, b. 1838, 9 mo. 4.
1480. Amos Casner, b. 1841, 4 mo. 27.
1481. Alexander Howell Casner, b. 1843, 3 mo. 23.
1482. John Casner, b. 1845, 5 mo. 25.
1483. Elizabeth Casner, b. 1848, 4 mo. 6.
1484. Enos Casner, b. 1851, 2 mo. 2.
1485. Clinton Casner, b. 1853, 8 mo. 21, d. 1864, 4 mo. 16.
1486. Caroline Casner, b. 1857, 6 mo. 7.
1487. William Casner, b. 1858, 3 mo. 27, d. 1877, 11 mo. 22.
1488. Annie Casner, b. 1861, 5 mo. 18.

(Amos[5], Benjamin[4], Henry[3], William[2], William[1].)

(549.) Jane Carver[6]—another daughter of Amos Carver and Elizabeth Lewis, his wife—was born 1823, 10th month 19; married 1846, 10th month 29, Jacob Leatherman, and resides in Plumstead Twp. Her children are:

1489. Etta P. Leatherman, b. 1847, 1 mo. 27.
1490. Zachary T. Leatherman, b. 1848, 10 mo. 20.
1491. Charles P. Leatherman, b. 1851, 5 mo. 5.
1492. R. Lizzie Leatherman, b. 1853, 9 mo. 27.
1493. Della P. Leatherman, b. 1860, 6 mo. 11.
1494. Anna B. Leatherman, b. 1863, 1 mo. 16, d. 1882, 11 mo. 20.

(Amos[5], Benjamin[4], Henry[3], William[2], William[1].)

(550.) Samuel Carver[6]—another son of Amos Carver and Elizabeth Lewis, his wife—was born in Plumstead Twp, Pa., 1826, 3d month; married Sarah Kegan of Hunterdon, N. J. His children are:

1495. J. Watson Carver, b. 1856.
1496. Amos Carver, b. 1858.

WILLIAM CARVER

(Amos[6], Benjamin[4], Henry[3], William[2], William[1].)

(551.) Caroline Carver[6]—another daughter of Amos Carver and Elizabeth Lewis, his wife—was born 1828, 3d month 22; married in 1848, 9th month 12, Joseph Fenton Caffee, and died 1880, 6th month 15, leaving children:

1497. Rachel Ann Caffee, b. 1849, 3 mo. 3.
1498. Ralph A. Caffee, b. 1851, 9 mo. 17.
1499. Mordecai C. Caffee, 1854, 10 mo. 11.
1500. Mary Eliza Caffee, b. 1859, 11 mo. 22, d. 1861, 9 mo. 30.
1501. Theodore B. Caffee, b. 1860, 8 mo. 29.
1502. Laura Matilda Caffee, b. 1863, 8 mo. 20.
1503. Sarah Jane Caffee, b. 1865, 6 mo. 7.

(552.) Mary Carver—another daughter of Amos Carver and Elizabeth Lewis, his wife—went to Canada. Know nothing.

(Amos[6], Benjamin[4], Henry[3], William[2], William[1].)

(553.) Lewis Carver[6]—another son of Amos Carver and Elizabeth Lewis, his wife—was born 1832, 10th month 13; married Diana Sherman, 1853, 10th month 6, and lives in Kingwood, N. J. Has children:

1504. Anna E. Carver, b. 1854, 7 mo. 15.
1505. Sarah Jane Carver, b. 1856, 11 mo. 16.
1506. Martha C. Carver, b. 1860, 2 mo. 14.
1507. William S. Carver, b. 1867, 3 mo. 19.
1508. Emma Carver, b. 1869, 10 mo. 16.

(Amos[6], Benjamin[4], Henry[3], William[2], William[1].)

(554.) Ruth Ann Carver[6]—another daughter of Amos Carver and Elizabeth Lewis, his wife—was born 1835, 2nd month 8; married 1854, 5th month 18, Jesse D. Carey, son of Enoch and Martha, was born in Plumstead Twp, 1830, 7th month 19. They reside in Watseka, Ill. Have children:

1509. Mary Martha Carey, b. 1858, 10 mo. 9.
1510. Jennie Elizabeth Carey, b. 1860, 12 mo. 3.
1511. Georgiana Carey, b. 1868, 1 mo. 3.

(555.) William Carver[6]—a son of William Carver and wife—was born in Berks Co., Pa. Know nothing.

(556.) Thomas Carver[6]—another son of William Carver and wife—was born in Berks Co., Pa.

(557.) Levi Carver[6]—another son of William Carver and wife—was born in Berks Co., Pa.

(558.) ——— Carver[6]—another child of William Carver and wife—was born in Berks Co., Pa.

(Jesse[5], Benjamin[4], Henry[3], William[2], William[1].)

(559.) Alfred Carver[6]—a son of Jesse Carver and Euphemia Ely, his wife—was born 1827, 10th month 12; married Catharine Ann Omer, 1853, 2d month 22, and resides in Martinsville, Morgan Co., Ind. Have children:

1512. George O. Carver, b. 1854, 1 mo. 4.
1513. Lizzie A. Carver, b. 1856, 6 mo. 13.
1514. Jessie A. Carver, b. 1859, 1 mo. 11.
1515. Elmer E. Carver, b. 1861, 8 mo. 11.
1516. Bertha A. Carver, b. 1864, 7 mo. 31.
1517. Nellie T. Carver, b. 1867, 9 mo. 18.
1518. John C. Carver, b. 1870, 4 mo. 30.
1519. Charles G. Carver, b. 1872, 12 mo. 5.
1520. Grace A. Carver, b. 1877, 3 mo. 11.

(Jesse[5], Benjamin[4], Henry[3], William[2], William[1].)

(560.) Samuel S. Carver[6]—another son of Jesse Carver and Euphemia Ely, his wife—was born in Bucks Co., Pa., 1830, 12th month 20; married Amanda D. Quick, 1858, 6th month 4, and resides in Hopewell, N. J. Has one child:

1521. Harry N. Carver.

(Jesse[5], Benjamin[4], Henry[3], William[2], William[1].)

(561.) Cynthia A. Carver[6]—a daughter of Jesse Carver and Euphemia Ely, his wife—was born in Bucks Co., Pa., 1833, 8th month 8; married George W. Rice of New Hope, Pa., 1851, 11th month 8, and resides in Trenton, N. J. Have children:

1521½. Emma A. Rice, b. in Lambertville, N. J., 1852, 9 mo. 5.
1522. Addie A. Rice, b. in Lambertville, N. J., 1857, 2 mo. 25.
1523. Mary E. Rice, b. in Lambertville, N. J., 1859, 7 mo. 24.
1524. George E. Rice, b. in Lambertville, N. J., 1861, 3 mo. 16.
1525. Theressa W. Rice, b. in Lambertville, N. J., 1865, 5 mo. 16.

(Jesse[5], Benjamin[4], Henry[3], William[2], William[1].)

(562.) Sophia Carver[6]—another daughter of Jesse Carver and Euphemia Ely, his wife—was born in Hunterdon Co., N. J., 1837, 4th month 24; married John Wright, 1854, 3d month 4, and resides in Trenton, N. J. Have children:

1526. Samuel C. Wright, b. in Lambertville, N. J., 1855, 2 mo. 25.
1527. Euphemia A. Wright, b. in Lambertville, N. J., 1857, 10 mo. 19.
1528. Elmer E. Wright, b. in Lambertville, N. J., 1861, 6 mo. 27.
1529. George B. Wright, b. in Lambertville, N. J., 1864, 1 mo. 1.
1530. Alfred E. Wright, b. in Lambertville, N. J., 1871, 8 mo. 16.

WILLIAM CARVER

(Jesse[5], Benjamin[4], Henry[3], William[2], William[1].)

(563.) Sophia Black[6]—a daughter of Cynthia Carver and Isaac Black, her husband—was born 1818, 4th month 12; married 1839, 5th month 15, Heil Wood. Her children are:

1531. Elvina Wood, b. 1840, 4 mo. 12, d. 1842, 11 mo. 3.
1532. Iris C. Wood, b. 1841, 10 mo. 3.
1533. Jane C. Wood, b. 1845, 9 mo. 14, d. 1856, 10 mo. 11.
1534. Jonathan B. Wood, b. 1847, 9 mo. 9.
1535. Isaac B. Wood, b. 1849, 11 mo. 14.
1536. Henry M. Wood, b. 1851, 9 mo. 25.
1537. Heil Wood, b. 1853, 10 mo. 1, d. 1866, 12 mo. 3.
1538. Sophia Wood, b. 1854, 10 mo. 21.
1539. Cynthia E. Wood, b. 1857, 12 mo. 2, d. 1871, 1 mo. 28.
1540. Catharine E. Wood, b. 1858, 12 mo. 2.
1541. Windfield S. Wood, b. 1861, 1 mo. 29.

(564.) Sarah Ann Black—another daughter of Cynthia Carver and Isaac Black, her husband—was born 1820, 11th month 20, died 1823, 12th month 16.

(565.) William Black—a son of Cynthia Carver and Isaac Black, her husband—was born 1823, 1st month 5; married 1848, 1st month 22, Isabella Althouse. Children:

1542. Alonzo Black, b. 1850, 12 mo. 18.
1543. Herman J. Black, b. 1853, 9 mo. 23, d. 1854, 12 mo. 7.
1544. Melissa M. Black, b. 1856, 9 mo. 12.
1545. William H. Black, b. 1859, 4 mo. 19.
1546. E. Anna Black, b. 1860, 8 mo. 30, d. 1882, 6 mo. 25.
1547. Jesse M. Black, b. 1861, 11 mo. 7.
1548. Abraham Black, b. 1864, 6 mo. 24.
1549. Sarah A. Black, b. 1867, 10 mo. 12.
1550. Arian Black, b. 1869, 9 mo. 7.
1551. John W. Black, b. 1874, 10 mo. 8.

(566.) Catharine Black—another daughter of Cynthia Carver and Isaac Black, her husband—was born 1825, 2nd month 6, died 1845, 2nd month 29. Not married.

(567.) Ann Elizabeth Black—another daughter of Cynthia Carver and Isaac Black, her husband—was born 1827, 12th month 13; married 1853, 1st month 1, Joseph G. Rice. They lived in Carversville, Pa. Both are dead; she died before her husband. No children.

(568.) Levi Black—another son of Cynthia Carver and Isaac Black, her husband—was born 1829, 12th month 28; married 1853, 1st month 6, Amanda Large. Their children are:

1552. Harriet Ella Black, b. 1853, 10 mo. 24.
1553. Anna M. Black, b. 1855, 9 mo. 20.
1554. Caroline P. Black, b. 1858, 11 mo. 6.
1555. Pennington Black, b. 186–, 1 mo. 20, d. 1868, 10 mo. 31.
1556. Stella Black, b. 1867, 4 mo. 8.

(Cynthia[5], Benjamin[4], Henry[3], William[2], William[1].)

(569.) Isaac C. Black[6]—another son of Cynthia Carver and Isaac Black, her husband—was born 1831, 9th month 26; married 1858, 7th month 8, Mira Simpson. His children are:

1557. Anna Estella Black, b. 1859, 8 mo. 17, d. 1863, 3 mo. 15.
1558. Ada D. Black, b. 1861, 2 mo. 27.
1559. Millie R. Black, b. 1862, 12 mo. 9, d. 1880, 9 mo. 15.
1560. Louis Black, b. 1861, 10 mo. 15.
1561. Joseph Black, b. 1866, 9 mo. 6.
1562. Bertha Black, b. 1868, 9 mo. 10, d. 1881, 3 mo. 10.

(Cynthia[5], Benjamin[4], Henry[3], William[2], William[1].)

(570.) Ezra W. Black[6]—another son of Cynthia Carver and Isaac Black, her husband—was born 1833, 10th month 16; married 1864, 12th month 25, Sarah Ann Murray. She died leaving four children, and he married, second time, 1875, 3d month 3, Margery Lambert, and had by her two children:

1563. Oliver Black, b. 1865, 10 mo. 11.
1567. Hannah Black, b. 1867, 6 mo. 27, d. 1869, 3 mo. 27.
1568. Pennington L. Black, b. 1869, 7 mo. 24, d. 1870, 12 mo. 22.
1569. Franklin Black, b. 1872, 1 mo. 1.
1570. Elizabeth L. Black, b. 1876, 12 mo. 24, by second wife.
1571. Carey Black, b. 1878, 1 mo. 14, by second wife.

First wife, Sarah Ann, died 1873, 6th month 9.

(571.) Abraham Black—another son of Cynthia Carver and Isaac Black, her husband—born 1836, 5th month 12. He was Colonel of the 14th New Jersey Volunteers in the War of the Rebellion, and killed at the Battle of the Wilderness, 1864, 5th month 12. Not married.

WILLIAM CARVER

(Cynthia[5], Benjamin[4], Henry[3], William[2], William[1].)

(572.) Jesse L. Black —another son of Cynthia Carver and Isaac Black, her husband—was born 1838, 8th month 23; married Sarah C. Carver, daughter of Isaac, 1865, 3d month 10. They had two children:

1572. Charles Black, b. 1866, 7 mo. 5.
1573. Della Black.

(573.) Jane Eliza Cole Fly—a daughter of Rachel Carver and Anthony Fly, her husband—was born in Solebury, Pa., 1824, 1st month 25; married Thomas Cooper Walton, 1850, 1st month 30. She resides at Clinton, N. J., where her husband died 1872, 10th month 11. Had children:

1574. Emma Augusta Walton, b. 1850, 11 mo. 7.
1575. Josephine Elton Walton, b. 1853, 8 mo. 22.
1576. Horace Mann Walton, b. 1857, 12 mo. 1.
1577. Martha Evans Walton, b. 1859, 9 mo. 24.
1578. Lucius Leedom Walton, b. 1865, 7 mo. 18.

(Rachel[5], Benjamin[4], Henry[3], William[2], William[1].)

(574.) Wilamina Maria Fly[6]—another daughter of Rachel Carver and Anthony Fly, her husband—was born in Solebury Twp, Pa., 1826, 8th month 17, died 1828, 1st month 25.

(575.) Levinia Fly—another daughter of Rachel Carver and Anthony Fly, her husband—was born in Solebury Twp, Pa., 1827, 3d month 7, died 1827, 11th month 22.

(576.) Isaac Otis Fly—a son of Rachel Carver and Anthony Fly, her husband—was born in Solebury Twp, Bucks Co., Pa., 1828, 12th month 21, died 1829, 4th month 16.

(577.) Sarah Ann Fly—another daughter of Rachel Carver and Anthony Fly, her husband—was born in Solebury Twp, Pa., 1830, 11th month 27, died 1837, 1st month 18.

(Rachel[5], Benjamin[4], Henry[3], William[2], William[1].)

(578.) Martha B. Fly[6]—another daughter of Rachel Carver and Anthony Fly, her husband—was born in Solebury, 1833, 11th month 11; married James Judson Evans, 1856, 3d month 13, and died 1859, 5th month 21. She had one child, a daughter:

1579. Ida Jane Evans, b. 1858, 1 mo. 15, d. 1858, 3 mo. 14.

(579.) Caroline Fly—another daughter of Rachel Carver and Anthony Fly, her husband—was born in Solebury, 1836, 1st month 9, died 1837, 1st month 20.

(Rachel[5], Benjamin[4], Henry[3], William[2], William[1].)

(580.) Mary H. Fly[6]—another daughter of Rachel Carver and Anthony Fly, her husband—was born in Solebury, 1873, 4th month 18; married James Judson Evans (being his second wife) in 1862, 1st month 16, and resides in Philadelphia City, Pa. Has children:

1580. Martha Evans, b. 1863, 12 mo. 18.
1581. Harriet Carlton Evans, b. 1866, 7 mo. 19.

(581.) Elizabeth Ann Fly—another daughter of Rachel Carver and Anthony Fly, her husband—was born in Solebury, 1839, 11th month 26, died 1874, 6th month 15. Not married.

(582.) Joseph Carver Fly—another son of Rachel Carver and Anthony Fly, her husband—was born in Solebury Twp, 1842, 1st month 1. Not married.

(583.) Rachel Carver Fly—another daughter of Rachel Carver and Anthony Fly, her husband—was born in Solebury Twp, Pa., 1847, 7th month 14. Not married.

(Levi[5], Benjamin[4], Henry[3], William[2], William[1].)

(584.) Mary Ann Carver[6]—a daughter of Levi Carver and Harriet Cosner, his wife—married William Reading. Have three children:

1582. Louisa Reading, d.
1583. William Reading, d.
1584. Anna Mary Reading.

(Levi[5], Benjamin[4], Henry[3], William[2], William[1].)

(585.) Lucinda Carver[6]—another daughter of Levi Carver and Harriet Cosner, his wife—was born 1828, 11th month 29. Not married.

(586.) Elias Carver—a son of Levi Carver and Harriet Cosner, his wife—was born 1836, 12th month 29; married Mary Ann Crothers. Has children:

1585. John W. Carver, d.
1586. William Carver.
1587. Anna B. Carver.
1588. Harry B. Carver.
1589. George S. Carver.
1590. Willet G. Carver.
1591. Stephen T. Carver.
1592. Edmund Carver, d.
1593. Elizabeth G. Carver.
1594. Levi Carver.

WILLIAM CARVER

(Levi[5], Benjamin[4], Henry[3], William[2], William[1].)

(587.) Rebecca Jane Carver[6]—another daughter of Levi Carver and Harriet Cosner, his wife—was born 1837, 3d month 9; married Stephen Tomlinson. She is now a widow and lives in Langhorn Boro, Pa. Had children:

1595. Harriet S. Tomlinson.
1596. Wilmer Tomlinson.
1597. Martha M. Tomlinson.
1598. Mary Emma Tomlinson.
1599. John C. Tomlinson.
1600. Lucy C. Tomlinson.
1601. Ida M. Tomlinson.
1602. Herbert Tomlinson.
1603. Charles Tomlinson.

(Levi[5], Benjamin[4], Henry[3], William[2], William[1].)

(588.) John W. Carver[6]—another son of Levi Carver and Harriet Cosner, his wife—was born 1839, 3d month 6; married 1868, 1st month 16, Phebe Ann Ashton, daughter of George W. of New Hope. She was born in 1844, 12th month 1. Had children:

1604. Preston C. Carver, b. 1869, 2 mo. 25.
1605. Caroline S. Carver, b. 1870, 3 mo. 23.

(589.) Sarah E. Carver—another daughter of Levi Carver and Harriet Cosner, his wife—was born 1841, 4th month 11. Died young.

(590.) Louisa Carver—another daughter of Levi Carver and Harriet Cosner, his wife—was born 1843, 9th month 3; married Thomas H. Delany, son of Uriah of Newtown, Pa. No children.

(591.) Rachel Carver—another daughter of Levi Carver and Harriet Cosner, his wife—was born 1845, 10th month 30; married Isaiah Hubbard, 1868, 11th month. Their children are:

1606. Arcurious Hubbard, d.
1607. Elizabeth Hubbard.
1608. William H. Hubbard, d.

(592.) Johanna Carver—another daughter of Levi Carver and Harriet Cosner, his wife—was born 1847, 11th month 2; married James A. Milnor, 1868, 12th month 25. Have one child:

1609. Elmira C. Milnor, b. 1870, 6 mo. 30.

(593.) Elmira Carver—another daughter of Levi Carver and Harriet Cosner, his wife—was born 1848, 2nd month 29; married Walter J. Smith of Germantown, Pa. Had children:

1610. Carl Smith.
1611. Elizabeth Smith.

(594.) William Carver—another son of Levi Carver and Harriet Cosner, his wife—was born 1852, 3d month 19; died young.

(Isaac[5], Benjamin[4], Henry[3], William[2], William[1].)

(595.) George W. Carver[6]—a son of Isaac and Elizabeth C. Biddle, his wife—was born in Philadelphia, 1836, 9th month 16; married Phebe C. Bowen, 1857, 3d month 19, and resides in Reading, Pa. Had children:

1612. Isaac K. Carver, b. 1857, 11 mo. 23, d. 1860, 10 mo. 10.
1613. Joseph Carver, b. 1861, 3 mo. 18, d. 1865, 3 mo. 24.
1614. Elizabeth Carver, b. 1864, 2 mo. 15.
1615. Charles C. Carver, b. 1868, 10 mo. 24.
1616. William E. S. Carver, b. 1872, 3 mo. 19.

(Isaac[5], Benjamin[4], Henry[3], William[2], William[1].)

(596.) Mary B. Carver[6]—a daughter of Isaac Carver and Elizabeth C. Biddle, his wife—was born in Philadelphia, 1838, 11th month 5; married William H. McLean, 1858, 11th month 7, and had two children. He died in 1862, 8th month 9. She then married Edward J. Springer, 1869, 11th month 28.

1617. Ida E. McLean, b. 1859, 8 mo. 5.
1618. Harry C. McLean, b. 1861, 8 mo. 7.

(597.) Charles C. Carver—another son of Isaac Carver and Elizabeth C. Biddle, his wife—was born 1841, 7th month 7, died 1863, 1st month 25, childless.

(Isaac[5], Benjamin[4], Henry[3], William[2], William[1].)

(598.) Sarah C. Carver[6]—another daughter of Isaac Carver and Elizabeth C. Biddle, his wife—was born 1844, 1st month 27; married Jesse L. Black, 1865, 3d month 10. Had two children.
See (572), page 105, as to children.

(599.) Emma T. Carver—another daughter of Isaac Carver and Elizabeth C. Biddle, his wife—was born 1846, 9th month 14. Not married.

(600.) Anna E. Carver—another daughter of Isaac Carver and Elizabeth C. Biddle, his wife—was born 1849, 6th month 12, died 1860, 6th month 4.

(601.) Henry C. Carver—another son of Isaac Carver and Elizabeth C. Biddle, his wife—was born 1852, 6th month 6, died 1860, 11th month 20.

WILLIAM CARVER

(602.) Davis W. Carver—another son of Isaac Carver and Elizabeth C. Biddle, his wife—was born 1855, 7th month 9, died 1860, 9th month 21.

(Miranda⁵, Benjamin⁴, Henry³, William², William¹.)

(603.) John Huey⁶—a son of Miranda Carver and George Huey, her husband—was born in Solebury Twp, Pa.; married Felicia Livezey, daughter of Cyrus, in 1858. He died in 1862 in Solebury Twp, Bucks Co., Pa. Had children:

1619. Caroline Huey.
1620. William Huey.

(604.) Edward Johnson—a son of Mary Carver and William Johnson—was born 1835, 5th month 8; married Rachel S. Walker, daughter of John, 1859, 2nd month 28. Had children:

1621. Lama Johnson, b. 1859, 12 mo. 15, d. 1861, 12 mo. 25.
1622. Phebe Johnson, b. 1861, 7 mo. 5.
1623. Charles N. Johnson, b. 1865, 3 mo. 26.
1624. William N. Johnson, b. 1868, 4 mo. 16.

(605.) George W. Johnson—another son of Mary Carver and William Johnson, her husband—was born 1841, 12th month 12, died unmarried.

(606.) Caroline Johnson—a daughter of Mary Carver and William Johnson—was born 1836, 3d month 29; married Joseph C. Harvey, 1862, 10th month, died 1863, 8th month 2. No children.

(607.) Phebe A. Johnson—another daughter of Mary Carver and William Johnson—was born 1839, 11th month 11, died 1859, 7th month 1. Not married.

(Mary⁵, Benjamin⁴, Henry³, William², William¹.)

(608.) William E. Johnson—another son of Mary Carver and William Johnson, her husband—was born 1845, 1st month 18; married Susanna H. Kitchen, daughter of William. Their children are:

1625. Victoria H. Johnson, b. 1871, 8 mo. 29.
1626. Flora M. Johnson, b. 1872, 11 mo. 3.
1627. Claude A. Johnson, b. 1874, 12 mo. 29.
1628. Orville C. Johnson, b. 1876, 3 mo. 17.
1629. Burley J. Johnson, b. 1878, 9 mo. 10.
1630. Mary L. Johnson, b. 1882, 11 mo. 23.

William E. Johnson died in April, 1886.

(609.) Jesse Black—a son of Elizabeth Carver and Abraham Black, her husband—was twice married: first, to Elizabeth W. Carver, daughter of David of Solebury (see children by this marriage, No. 478). She died about 1853 or 1854; and Jesse married, secondly, Anna Small, 1855, 11th month 3, and died in July, 1882. His children by this marriage are:

1631. William S. Black, b. 1856, 7 mo. 30, d.
1632. Horace W. Black, b. 1858, 8 mo. 25, d.
1633. Kirk Black, b. 1862, 8 mo. 28.
1634. Ann Elizabeth Black, b. 1868, 6 mo. 8.

(610.) Julia Black—a daughter of Elizabeth Carver and Abraham Black, her husband—died unmarried.

(611.) Sarah E. Black—another daughter of Elizabeth Carver and Abraham Black, her husband—was born 1818, 3d month 15; married Caleb Evans, and were living at Carversville, Pa. Her children are:

1635. Wilson C. Evans, b. 1838, 1 mo. 23.
1636. Mary Emma Evans, b. 1848, 11 mo. 19.

(612.) Henry Black—another son of Elizabeth Carver and Abraham Black, her husband.

(613.) Benjamin Black—another son of Elizabeth Carver and Abraham Black, her husband—died leaving five or six children.

(614.) Kirk Black—another son of Elizabeth Carver and Abraham Black, her husband—married Phebe White, daughter of William. He died 1859, leaving one child:

1637. William Black, b. 1857.

(615.) Elizabeth F. Black—another daughter of Elizabeth Carver and Abraham Black, her husband—was born 1830, 7th month 20; married 1850, 2nd month 27, William Bellemere, and lives in Philadelphia. Children:

1638. Emily Adell Bellemere, b. 1851, 3 mo. 14, d. 1854, 1 mo. 15.
1639. Henry Kirk Bellemere, b. 1853, 9 mo. 18, d. 1859, 11 mo. 22.
1640. John Francis Bellemere, b. 1855. 12 mo. 24.
1641. William H. Bellemere, b. 1859, 12 mo. 20, d. 1860, 8 mo. 5.
1642. Charles H. M. Bellemere, b. 1865, 2 mo. 7.

(616.) Rebecca J. Black—another daughter of Elizabeth Carver and Abraham Black—was born 1832, 11th month 14, died 1835, 10th month 9.

(617.) Eli Black—another son of Elizabeth Carver and Abraham Black, her husband—married Sarah Ann Ely. Had children:

1643. Abraham Black, b. 1864, d. 1882.
1644. Sarah Ann Black, b. 1868.
1645. Henry Black, b. 1870.
1646. Benjamin Black, b. 1874.

(618.) Mary Black—another daughter of Elizabeth Carver and Abraham Black, her husband—married Alfred Firman; he died intestate, fore-part of October, 1878. Had children:

1647. Caleb Firman, } Twins.
1648. Eli Firman,
1649. Sarah Firman.
1650. Letitia Firman.

(619.) Marsella Harrold—a daughter of William Harrold and Margaret Jones—died in infancy.

(620.) Minnie Harrold—another child of William Harrold and Margaret Jones—died at about 18 years.

(620½.) Oliver Harrold—another son of William Harrold and Margaret Jones—died in infancy.

(621.) Alfred Harrold—another child of William Harrold and Margaret Jones, his wife—was born in Ohio, 1844, 8th month 6, was killed in the War of the Rebellion at the battle of Stony River, 1862, 12th month 31. He was a Private in Company C, 74th Volunteer Infantry, Colonel Moody commanding.

(622.) Maria Harrold—a daughter of William Harrold and Margaret Jones, his wife—married in London, England, 1878, 8th month, Prof. H. D. Garrison, now of Douglas University, Chicago. Has no children.

(623.) Emma Harrold—another daughter of William Harrold and Margaret Jones, his wife—married L. C. Irren, a merchant of South Charleston, Ohio. She is the youngest. No children.

(William[5], David[4], Rachel[3], William[2], William[1].)

(624.) Annie Harrold—another daughter of William Harrold and Margaret Jones, his wife—married Wells Trader of Minneapolis, Minn. Has children:

1651. Harrold Trader, b. 1879.
1652. Kitty Castle Trader, b. 1882.

GENEALOGY OF

(William[5], David[4], Rachel[3], William[2], William[1].)

(625.) Seymore Harrold—another son of William Harrold and Margaret Jones, his wife—was born in Ohio; married Laura Pierce, of the Pierces, near Kennett Square, Chester Co., Pa., and lives at South Charleston, Ohio, where he owns 700 acres of land, part of the Harrold Homestead. He spent 1878 and 1879 in Europe, and has the following children:

1653. Ralph Harrold, b. 1868, 11 mo. 1.
1654. Bertha Harrold, b. 1870, 10 mo. 13.
1655. Annie Harrold, b. 1877, 11 mo. 6.
1656. Helen Harrold, b. 1881, 8 mo. 17.

(Samuel H.[5], Rebecca[4], Rachel[3], William[2], William[1].)

(626.) Fanny E. Gillingham[6]—a daughter of Samuel H. Gillingham and Lucy L. Eddy, his wife—was born 1827, 10th month 12; married Jared Kibbee, of Port Huron, 1852, 3d month 23. Have children:

1657. Ada F. Kibbee.
1658. Lucy E. Kibbee.
1659. Samuel H. Kibbee.
1660. Henry C. Kibbee.
1661. Eleanor P. Kibbee.
1662. Fanny L. Kibbee.

(627.) Joseph E. Gillingham—a son of Samuel H. Gillingham and Lucy L. Eddy, his wife—was born in Philadelphia, 1830, 7th month 5; married Clara Donaldson in 1864. Know nothing more.

(Samuel[5], Rebecca[4], Rachel[3], William[2], William[1].)

(628.) Lewis H. Gillingham[6]—another son of Samuel H. Gillingham and Lucy L. Eddy, his wife—was born in Philadelphia, 1836, 7th month 3; married 1859, 6th month 12, Louisa M. Bartle. Has children:

1863. William Gillingham, b. 1860, 5 mo. 9.
1864. Hattie Gillingham.

(629.) Frank C. Gillingham—born 1840, 4th month 14, of Samuel H. and Louisa M. Hubbs, his second wife—married Tacey Morris of New Jersey. No children.

(630.) Rebecca H. Gilpin—a daughter of Ann Gillingham and Joseph F. Gilpin, her husband—was born 1834, 3d month 21; married Firman Rogers, 1856, 1st month 24.

(Samuel H.[5], Rebecca[4], Rachel[3], William[2], William[1].)

(631.) George Gilpin[6]—a son of Ann Gillingham and Joseph F. Gilpin, her husband—was born 1838, 12th month 21; married 1872, 12th month 3, Sarah C. Winsten of New York City. Has one child:

1865. Anna Gilpin.

WILLIAM CARVER

(632.) Anna Frances Buckman—a daughter of Emmaline L. Gillingham and Dilworth Buckman, her husband—was born 1844, 1st month 17.

(633.) Caroline L. Buckman—another daughter of Emmaline L. Gillingham and Dilworth Buckman, her husband—was born 1841, 1st month 31.

(634.) S. Harrold Buckman—a son of Emmaline L. Gillingham and Dilworth Buckman, her husband—was born 1855, 1st month 6.

(635.) William Shaw—a son of Sarah Carver and Samuel Shaw, her husband—not married.

(636.) Allen Shaw—another son of Sarah Carver and Samuel Shaw, her husband—not married.

(637.) A daughter of Sarah Carver and Samuel Shaw, her husband—died young.

(638.) Edward Boyer—a son of Sarah Carver and Henry Boyer, her second husband.

(639.) Edward E. Carver—a son of William Carver and Mary E. McAdams—married Hannah Vansant.

(640.) Mary Emma Carver—a daughter of William Carver and Mary E. McAdams—deceased.

(William[6], Israel[5], William[4], William[3], William[2], William[1].)
(641.) Charles H. Carver[7]—another son of William Carver and Mary E. McAdams, his wife.

(642.) Elmer E. Carver—another son of William Carver and Mary E. McAdams, his wife.

(643.) ———— Carver—a son of David Carver and Caroline Stradling, his wife—was born about 1869.

(Deborah[6], Israel[5], William[4], William[3], William[2], William[1].)
(644.) Flora Z. Lewis[7]—a daughter of Deborah E. Carver and William Lewis, her husband—was born 1859, 2nd month 20.

(645.) Ida M. Lewis—a daughter of Deborah E. Carver and William Lewis, her husband—was born 1861, 4th month 5; died 1868, 8th month 20.

(646.) Howard A. Lewis—a son of Deborah E. Carver and William Lewis, her husband—was born 1863, 6th month 1.

(647.) Fannie S. Lewis—another daughter of Deborah E. Carver and William Lewis, her husband—was born 1866, 4th month 19.

(648.) Evan T. Lewis—another son of Deborah E. Carver and William Lewis, her husband—was born 1868, 12th month 12.

(649.) Sallie W. Lewis—another daughter of Deborah E. Carver and William Lewis, her husband—was born 1871, 3d month 6.

(650.) Franklin H. Lewis—another son of Deborah E. Carver and William Lewis, her husband—was born 1878, 2nd month 3.

(Mary[6], Israel[5], William[4], William[3], William[2], William[1].)

(651.) Frank Miller[7]—a son of Mary Carver and Samuel W. Miller, her husband—was born 1852, 8th month 1.

(652.) William E. Miller—another son of Mary Carver and Samuel W. Miller, her husband—was born 1857, 10th month 16, died 1865, 7th month 26.

(653.) Carrie Miller—a daughter of Mary Carver and Samuel W. Miller, her husband—was born 1861, 1st month 27.

(Strickland[6], Israel[5], William[4], William[3], William[2], William[1].)

(654.) Kirk Carver[7]—a son of Strickland Carver and Asenath White, his wife—married Mary Morgan 1872, 11th month 30. His children are:

1866. Annie Carver.
1868. George Carver.
1868. William Carver.
1869. Bertha Carver.
1870. Herbert Carver.
1871. Letitia Carver.
1872. Chester Carver.
1873. Ada Carver, d. 1884, 9 mo. 3, æt. 7 mo.

(Strickland[6], Israel[5], William[4], William[3], William[2], William[1].)

(655.) Mary Carver[7]—a daughter of Strickland Carver and Asenath White, his wife—married Amos Bennett of Buckingham. Had children:

1874. Harry Bennett.
1875. ———— Bennett.

(Strickland[6], Israel[5], William[4], William[3], William[2], William[1].)

(656.) Matilda Carver[7]—another daughter of Strickland Carver and Asenath White, his wife—married Moore Bennett. Have children:

1876. Stephen Bennett.
1877. Miles Bennett.
1878. ———— Bennett, a daughter.

(657.) Maria White—a daughter of Lydia Carver and Amos White, her husband—was born in Buckingham, Pa.

(658.) David White—a son of Lydia Carver and Amos White, her husband—was born in Buckingham; married Mary C. Kirk.

(659.) Mary A. White—a daughter of Lydia Carver and Amos White, her husband—was born in Buckingham; married George Cosner.

(660.) Sarah White—another daughter of Lydia Carver and Amos White, her husband—was born in Buckingham; married Winfield Large.

(661.) Elizabeth White—another daughter of Lydia Carver and Amos White, her husband—was born in Buckingham Twp, Bucks Co., Pa.

(662.) Israel White—a son of Lydia Carver and Amos White, her husband—deceased.

(663.) Mary Ellen Reynolds—a daughter of Jane G. Carver and David Reynolds—her husband.

(664.) Harry Carver—a son of Theodore Carver and Sarah Bodine, her husband.

(665.) Theodore S. Carver—a son of Stephen Carver and Emily E. Keen, his wife.

(666.) Herbert L. Carver—another son of Stephen Carver and Emily E. Keen, his wife.

(667.) Annie K. Doan—a daughter of Mary Carver and Stephen K. Doan, his wife.

(Benjamin W.[6], Miles[5], William[4], William[3], William[2], William[1].)
(668.) Mary Emma Carver[7]—a daughter of Benjamin Watson Carver and Harriet Cooper—his wife.

(669.) Elmer Ellsworth Carver—a son of Thomas Ellwood Carver and Julia A. Tomlinson, his wife.

(James[6], Ann[5], William[4], William[3], William[2], William[1].)
(670.) George McDowell[7]—a son of James McDowell and Elizabeth Walton, his wife.

(671.) Henry McDowell—another son of James McDowell and Elizabeth Walton, his wife.

(672.) Caroline McDowell—a daughter of James McDowell and Elizabeth Walton—his wife.

(James[6], Ann[5], William[4], Willliam[3], William[2], William[1].)
(673.) Hannah McDowell[7]—another daughter of James McDowell and Elizabeth Walton, his wife.

(674.) Caroline Miller—a daughter of Margaret Carver and Reading Miller.

(675.) Adelaide Miller—another daughter of Margaret Carver and Reading Miller, her husband.

(676.) Kate Miller—another daughter of Margaret Carver and Reading Miller, her husband.

(677.) Anna Carver—a daughter of Thomas Early Carver and wife.

(Alfred[6], James[5], William[4], William[3], William[2], William[1].)
(716.) Wilhelmina Carver[7]—a daughter of Alfred S. Carver and Mary Paxson, his wife—was born in 1842; married Levi Means. She had a daughter and died in confinement. The daughter married Valentine Ruth. They had one son who died.

(717.) James Henry Carver—a son of Alfred S. Carver and Mary Slutter, his wife—was born in Hilltown Twp; married Mary Wambold, and have two sons:

1879. ———— Wambold.
1880. ———— Wambold.

(Alfred[6], James[5], William[4], William[3], William[2], William[1].)
(718.) Terissa Carver[7]—another daughter of Alfred S. Carver and Mary Slutter, his wife—married David D. Morgan, and died. Had one son:

1881. ———— Morgan.

(Paxson[6], James[5], William[4], William[3], William[2], William[1].)
(719.) Nathan C. Carver[7]—a son of Paxson Carver—was born 1846, 12th month 18; married Almira S. Cramer, 1870, 5th month 17. Children:

1882. Frank Carver, b. 1871, 1 mo. 8.
1883. Alfred Carver, b. 1874, 5 mo. 14.
1884. Lizzie Carver, b. 1878, 5 mo. 10.

WILLIAM CARVER

(Paxson⁶, James⁵, William⁴, William³, William², William¹.)

(720.) Joseph Ott Carver⁷—another son of Paxson Carver and Elizabeth K. Ott, his wife—was born 1848, 10th month 2; married Eliza P. Thornton, 1875, 12th month 18. Had children:

1885. Wilmer P. Carver, b. 1878, 4 mo. 13.
1885½. George P. Carver, b. 1880, 7 mo. 16, d. 1881, 3 mo. 5.
1886. Elmer Carver, b. 1881, 7 mo. 30.

(721.) Addie C. Carver—a daughter of Paxson Carver and Elizabeth K. Ott, his wife—was born 1851, 1st month 11; married Theodore P. White, 1874, 11th month 12. Had one child:

1886½. Howard W. White, b. 1876, 4 mo. 1, d. 1876, 7 mo. 12.

(722.) Emma B. Carver—another daughter of Paxson Carver and Elizabeth K. Ott, his wife—was born 1853, 1st month 15.

(723.) Susanna O. Carver—another daughter of Paxson Carver and Elizabeth K. Ott, his wife—was born 1857, 8th month 21, died 1860, 10th month 2.

(724.) Hannah K. Carver—another daughter of Paxson Carver and Elizabeth K. Ott, his wife—was born 1859, 10th month 27, died 1860, 10 month 7.

(725.) Catharine K. Carver—another daughter of Paxson Carver and Elizabeth K. Ott, his wife—born 1863, 9th month 17.

(Martha⁶, (Sarah⁵, William⁴, William³, William², William¹.)
(747.) Georgiene Atkinson⁷—a daughter of Martha B. Stradling and Jesse Atkinson, her husband.

(748.) William S. Atkinson⁷—a son of Martha B. Stradling and Jesse Atkinson, her husband.

(Martha⁶, Sarah⁵, William⁴, William³, William², William¹.)
(749.) Stephen K. Atkinson⁷—another son of Martha B. Stradling and Jesse Atkinson, her husband—was married, 1877, 5th month 24, Sarah Ruth, daughter of John. Had children:

1887. Elmer H. Atkinson.
1888. Martha Ruth Atkinson.

(Martha⁶, Sarah⁵, William⁴, William³, William², William¹.)
(750.) Sallie S. Atkinson⁷—a daughter of Martha B. Stradling and Jesse Atkinson, her husband—married Stewart C. Crome. Had children.

(Smith[6], Benjamin[5], William[4], William[3], William[2], William[1].)

(751.) Clara L. Carver[7]—a daughter of Smith Carver and Sarah E. Montgomery, his wife—was born 1876, 9th month 18.

(752.) Hannah M. Carver—another daughter of Smith Carver and Sarah E. Montgomery, his wife—was born 1869, 6th month 29.

(753.) Mattie B. Carver—another daughter of Smith Carver and Sarah E. Montgomery, his wife—was born 1872, 4th month 21.

(Hannah[6], Esther[5], William[4], William[3], William[2], William[1].)

(754.) Angelina Carver[7]—a daughter of Hannah McDowell and Joel Carver, her husband—was born 1842, 6th month 9, died 1742, 7th month 6.

(George[6], Esther[5], Joseph[4], William[3], William[2], William[1].)

(755.) A. Caroline McDowell[7]—a daughter of George McDowell and Amanda Mathews, his wife.

(George,[6] Esther[5], Joseph[4], William[3], William[2], William[1].)

(756.) Esther McDowell[7]—another daughter of George McDowell and Amanda Mathews, his wife—was born 1848, 4th month 26; married John C. Walton, 1870, 11th month 30.

(757.) William H. McDowell—a son of George McDowell and Amanda Mathews, his wife.

(George[6], Esther[5], Joseph[4], William[3], William[2], William[1].)

(758.) Kinsey McDowell[7]—another son of George McDowell and Amanda Mathews, his wife—married ——— Malone.

(759.) George McDowell—another son of George McDowell and Amanda Mathews, his wife.

(William[6], Esther[5], Joseph[4], William[3], William[2], William[1].)

(760.) Anna M. McDowell[7]—a daughter of William McDowell and Elenor Duer, his wife—was born 1843, 7th month 7.

(William[6], Esther[5], Joseph[4], William[3], William[2], William[1].)

(761.) Hannah McDowell[7]—a daughter of William McDowell and Elenor Duer, his wife—was born 1845, 9th month 4.

(762.) Clarissa McDowell—another daughter of William McDowell and Elenor Duer, his wife—was born 1849, 4th month 7, died 1850, 8th month 22.

WILLIAM CARVER

(Robert[6], Esther[5], William[4], William[3], William[2], William[1].)
(763.) William McDowell[7]—a son of Robert McDowell and Catharine Neff, his wife—deceased.

(Robert[6], Esther[5], William[4], William[3], William[2], William[1].)
(764.) Jennie McDowell[7]—a daughter of Robert McDowell and Catharine Neff, his wife—deceased.

(765.) Lettie McDowell—another daughter of Robert McDowell and Catharine Neff, his wife.

(Charles[6], Esther[5], Joseph[4], William[3], William[2], William[1].)
(767.) Hannah Ellen Blaker[7]—a daughter of Charles M. Blaker and Levina Lair, his wife—was born 1855, 11th month 14; married William C. Conover, 1875, 12th month 7. Had one child:

1889. Mary Conover, b. 1877, 4 mo. 4.

(768.) William Winfield Blaker—a son of Charles M. Blaker and Levina Lair, his wife—was born 1857, 7th month 18.

(Jane[6], Joseph[5], Joel[4], Joseph[3], William[2], William[1].)
(956.) Joseph C. Hibbs[7]—a son of Jane Carver and Benjamin Hibbs, her husband—was born 1819; married, 1843, 1st month 13, Ann Everett, by whom he had his children, she died in 1866. He then married Ellen Finney, daughter of Joseph. His childred are:

1890. Lizzie Hibbs.
1891. Mary Jane Hibbs.
1892. George Hibbs.
1893. Ann Hibbs.
1894. William A. Hibbs.
1895. Benjamin Hibbs, d. æt. 3 weeks.

(Jane[6], Joseph[5], Joel[4], Joseph[3], William[2], William[1].)
(957.) Sarah Ann Hibbs[7]—a daughter of Jane Carver and Benjamim Hibbs, her husband—married Henry C. Cornell, 1844, 12th month 25. She is a widow. Her husband died, 1833, 3d month 29, had one child:

1896. Jane Eliza Cornell, d. æt. 5 years.

(970.) Henry Q. Smith— a son of Elizabeth Carver and Mahlon Smith, her husband—was born in Wrightstown, Pa.; married Susan Buckman. Their children are:

1897. Elma Smith.
1898. William Smith.

(976.) Carrie Beans—a daughter of Ann Carver and Robert Beans—was born in Northampton Twp, Bucks Co.; married J. Warren Paxson.

(977.) Annie E. Beans—another daughter of Ann Carver and Robert Beans, her husband—married Frank Phillips, son of Charles. One child:

1899. Robert Beans Phillips.

(980.) Martha Smith—a daughter of Mary Carver and Carlile Smith, her husband—married Comly Woodman. Have children:

1900. Albert Woodman.
1901. Paul Woodman.
1902. Grace Woodman.

(981.) William Smith—a son of Mary Carver and Carlile Smith, married Sarah Twining. One child:

1903. Hannah Smith.

(985.) Enos Morris Lloyd—a son of John Lloyd and Amanda M. Morris, his wife—was born 1827, 7th month 10; married Julia Hendrie, daughter of William S. Hendrie, M. D. of Doylestown, in the fall of 1848. He studied law with Hon. John Fox and practiced in Doylestown from November 9th, 1848, the time he was admitted, till his death, 1874. He had two children:

1904. Henry A. Lloyd, Esq., attorney-at-law, b. 1849, 11 mo. 12.
1905. James D. Lloyd, M. D., b. 1851.

(986.) Henry C. Lloyd, M. D.—another son of John Lloyd and Amanda M. Morris, his wife—was born 1829; married in 1853, Emily Westhall of Texas. He was in the Medical Department of the University of Philadelphia, Pa., and graduated a M. D., July 3d, 1848. He died at Yardley, Pa., intestate, April 3d, 1889. Left a widow and children:

1906. Henry A. Lloyd, d. 1863.
1907. John M. Lloyd, d 1863.
1908. Enos Morris Lloyd, M. D.
1909. William Y. Lloyd.
1910. Amanda F. Lloyd.

(1004.) Enos B. Carver—a son of John J. Carver and Margaret Black, his wife—was born in Buckingham, and was twice married: first, to Patience Titus, daughter of Seruch, and secondly, to Elizabeth Kirk. His children are by his first wife:

1911. Titus Carver.
1912. Elizabeth Carver, m. Richard Carver.

(1011.) Cynthia Carver—a daughter of John J. Carver and Mary Black, his wife—married John Chittick. She died, leaving children:

1913. John Chittick.
1914. ———— Chittick.

(1017.) Samuel H. Carver—a son of James Carver and Louisa Hamilton, his wife, daughter of Benjamin—married Julia Ann Fryling, 1863, 12th month 10. His children are:

1915. Ella Carver.
1916. Lettie Carver.

(James[6], Joseph[5], John[4], Joseph[3], William[2], William[1].)
(1018.) Loretta Carver[7]—a daughter of James Carver and Louisa Hamilton, his wife, daughter of Benjamin—married 1873, 12th month 24, Edwin Yerkes. Their children are:

1917. Maggie Yerkes.
1918. John Yerkes.

(William[6], Joseph[5], John[4], Joseph[3], William[2], William[1].)
(1024.) Amy Carver[7]—a daughter of William Carver and Elmira Black, his wife—married John Ewer. One child:

1919. Elmira Ewer.

(Hannah[6], Joseph[5], John[4], Joseph[3], William[2], William[1].)
(1025.) Samuel Kirk[7]—a son of Hannah Carver and William R. Kirk, Esq., son of John, who came from Ireland—was born in Buckingham Twp, and married Sarah Worthington, 1867, 12th month 5. Have a child:

1920. Ella Kirk.

(1026.) William Kirk—another son of Hannah Carver and William R. Kirk, Esq., son of John, who came from Ireland—married 1868, 8th month 25, Hannah Black. Have children:

1921. Benjamin Kirk.
1922. Dorrie Kirk.

(1027.) Margaret Kirk—a daughter of Hannah Carver and William R. Kirk, Esq., son of John, who came from Ireland—married 1867, 9th month 22, Elisha Radcliff. Have a child:

1923. Samuel K. Radcliff.

(1028.) John Kirk—another son of Hannah Carver and William R. Kirk, Esq., son of John—married 1868, 10th month 8, Sarah Twining. Have children:

1924. Anna Kirk.
1925. Abbott Kirk.
1926. William Kirk.
1927. Mary Kirk.

(Hannah⁶, Joseph⁵, John⁴, Joseph³, William², William¹.)

(1029.) Mary Ellen Kirk⁷—another daughter of Hannah Carver and William R. Kirk, Esq., son of John, from Ireland—married 1867, 1st month 24, Chalkley Twining. Have a child:

1928. Joseph Twining.

(Mary Ann⁶, Joseph⁵, John⁴, Joseph³, William², William¹.)

(1031.) Audery Cosner⁷—a daughter of Mary Ann Carver and H. Morris Cosner, her husband—was born 1857, 7th month; married Henry Drake. Had children:

1929. Anna Drake.
1930. Adolphus Drake.
1931. Harry Drake.
1932. Mary Drake.

(Mary Ann⁶, Joseph⁵, John⁴, Joseph³, William², William¹.)

(1032.) Mary H. Cosner⁷—another daughter of Mary Ann Carver and H. Morris Cosner, her husband—was born in 1859; married Warner Peters. Has children:

1933. Esther Peters.
1934. Martha Peters.

(1041.) Sarah Jane Carver—a daughter of George W. Carver and Mary Ann Carey, his wife—was born 1846, 8th month 11; married 1868, 10th month 21, Richard Brown of Falsington, Pa. Had children:

1935. Susan J. Brown.
1936. William L. Brown.
1937. Howard C. Brown.

(1043.) Miranda Caroline Carver—another daughter of George W. Carver and Mary Ann Carey, his wife—born 1851, 2nd month 14; married, 1874, 12th month 1, Ellwood Hegburn. Has Children:

1938. John Hegburn.
1939. Lilian B. Hegburn.
1940. Minnie Hegburn.

(George⁶, Isaac⁵, Joseph⁴, Joseph³, William², William¹.)

(1045.) Ermina Virginia Carver⁷—another daughter of George W. Carver and Mary Ann Carey, his wife—was born 1856, 2nd month 27; married, 1878, 11th month 14, Walter Thompson. Has children:

1941. Harwood Thompson.
1942. Mary Thompson.

(1048.) Henry Williams—a son of Elizabeth A. Carver and Henry Williams, her husband—was born 1852, 11th month 7; married Rebecca March of Chester Co., Pa., 1879, 6th month 27, lives in Chicago. Has children:

1943. Henry Williams
1944. George M. Williams.
1945. Carver Williams.

(1049.) Charles F. Williams—another son of Elizabeth A. Carver and Henry Williams, her husband—was born 1856, 4th month 30. He was a printer, but subsequently studied for the ministry and became a Baptist Minister, residing in Montgomery Co., Pa. He was twice married: first, to Flora Christee of Chester Co., Pa., in 1881, 5th month 7, and had one child by her; secondly, he married in 1884, 3d month 27, Mary A. Lees, daughter of Joseph Lees of the firm of Lees & Son. His children are:

1945¼. J. Ambler Williams, b. 1881, 3 mo. 12.
1945½. J. Lees Williams, b. 1885, 1 mo. 11.

(John[6], John[5], John[4], Joseph[3], William[2], William[1].)

(1052.) Sarah H. Carver[7]—a daughter of John Carver and Mary E. Howell, his wife—was born in 1853, married Absalom Atchley in 1871. Children are:

1946. Lizzie Atchley.
1947. Ella Atchley.

(1053.) Harrison E. Carver—a son of John Carver and Mary E. Howell, his wife—was born in 1855; married Harriet Hampton in 1876. Has children:

1948. John Carver.
1949. Bertha Carver.
1950. Rachel Carver.

(Adin[6], John[5], John[4], Joseph[3], William[2], William[1].)

(1063.) Charles H. Carver—a son of Adin Carver and Sarah V. Howell, his wife—was born in 1851; married in 1873, Ann M. Baily. Has children:

1951. Anna Carver, b. 1874.
1952. Rachel Carver, b. 1877.
1953. Edward B. Carver, b. 1880.

(1064.) Mary A. Carver—a daughter of Adin Carver and Sarah V. Howell, his wife—was born in 1854; married George R. Miller, 1872. Has children:

1954. Nelson Miller, b. 1873.
1955. Adin Miller, b. 1875.
1956. Walter Miller, b. 1878.

(1074.) Alonzo L. Carver—a son of Oliver Carver and Sarah Hughes, his wife—was born in 1860—married Mary L. Woodruff in 1883, 8th month, 8. One child:

1957. Orville Ray Carver.

(1086.) Watson D. Trego—a son of Kesiah Carver and Allen Trego, her husband—married Elizabeth Wilkins in 1858. Have children:

1958. Rose Ella Trego.
1959. Edith L. Trego.
1960. Edgar W. Trego.
1961. Mary B. Trego.
1962. Abby B. Trego.
1963. Allen W. Trego.
1964. Nellie W. Trego.

(Kesiah^6, John^5, John^4, Joseph^3, William^2, William^1.)

(1087.) Mary E. Trego^7—a daughter of Kesiah Carver and Allen Trego, her husband—married Cyrus Ulam in 1862. Had one child:

1965. Rosa Nellie Ulam, who married in 1878, Robert J. McNally. Had children:
1966. Elizabeth S. McNally.
1967. Catharine McNally.

(1116.) Evelina Gilbert—a daughter of George W. Gilbert and Eliza Guinn, his first wife—married John C. Bloom at Norristown, Pa. One child:

1968. Harry D. Bloom.

(1117.) Theodore Gilbert—a son of George W. Gilbert and Eliza Guinn, his first wife—married Sarah Rowan. Have one child:

1969. Theodore Gilbert.

(1121.) Harriet Gilbert—a daughter of George W. Gilbert and Debbie Logan, his second wife—married John C. Lewis. Have children:

1970. Daniel Lewis.
1971. Harry Lewis.

(1120.) Ellwood Gilbert—another son of George W. Gilbert and Debbie Logan, his socond wife—married Annie Longstreth. Have children:

1972. Walter Gilbert.
1973. Annie Gilbert.

(1119.) Daniel Gilbert—another son of George W. Gilbert and Debbie Logan, his second wife—married Annie Biddle. Have one child:

1974. Ida Gilbert.

WILLIAM CARVER

(1122.) Mary Gilbert—another daughter of George W. Gilbert and Debbie Logan, his second wife—married Larry Ramsy. Had one child:

1975. ———— Ramsy.

(1126.) Watson Tomlinson Ward—a son of Lydia Ann Gilbert and John Ward, her husband—was born on Thursday, 1840, 4th month 2; married Eleanor DeWees, who was born Thursday, 1838, 9th month 13th. Their children are:

1976. Alfred R. Ward, b. 1865, 11 mo. 7.
1977. John Ward, b. 1867, 10 mo. 8.
1978. Gertrude Ward, b. 1870, 1 mo. 15.
1979. Anna J. Ward, b. 1872, 7 mo. 27.
1980. Ella D. Ward, b. 1875, 4 mo. 23.
1981. George H. Ward, b. 1877, 10 mo. 26, } Twins.
1982. Harry H. Ward, b. 1877, 10 mo. 26, }
1983. Lizzie B. Ward, b. 1880, 3 mo. 1.

(1130.) Edwin M. Gilbert—a son of John Gilbert and Mary Ann Wallace, his wife—was born 1846, 4th month 10. Has children:

1984. Nellie Gilbert, b. 1876, 2 mo. 29.
1985. Maggie Gilbert, b. 1879, 11 mo. 7.
1986. William Gilbert, b. 1881, 9 mo. 29.

(1131.) Ann M. Gilbert—a daughter of John Gilbert and Mary Wallace, his wife—was born 1838, 1st month 27; married Jacob E. Abbott, 1869, 12th month 15. Have children:

1987. Harry Abbott, b. 1870, 9 mo. 15.
1988. Anna L. Abbott, b. 1883, 9 mo. 20.

(1132.) John Howard Evans, M. D.—a son of Rebecca Gilbert and Joseph Evans, her husband—was born 1846, 1st month; married Mattie Kennady, daughter of Samuel, 1878, 3d month 7. Reside in Philadelphia. One child:

1989. Joseph Samuel Evans, b. 1848, 5 mo. 27.

(1146.) John Richard Clemons, Jr.—a son of Agnes Gilbert and Richard Clemons, her husband—was born 1857, 5th month 30; married Lizzie D. Young, 1880, 3d month 8. Have one child:

1990. Florence Clemons, b. 1880, 12 mo. 23.

GENEALOGY OF

(1149.) John Clarkson Addis—A son of John Carver Addis and Martha Ramsey Thomas, his wife—was born 1845, 7th month 14; married 1867, 7th month 10, Mary Anna Payne, she died 1883, 2nd month 25. His second wife was Fanny Supple. Had children:

1991. Romand L. Addis, b. 1868, 11 mo. 28, d. 1870, 11 mo. 26.
1992. Leonard Payne Addis, b. 1870, 11 mo. 26.
1993. Lavinia Gertrude Addis, b. 1872, 12 mo. 26.

(1167.) Miles M. Martindell—son of J. Warner Martindell—married Lizzie F. Engel of Prince George Co., Maryland. Have children:

1994. Harry E. Martindell, b. 1879, 12 mo. 20.
1995. Bertha A. Martindell, b. 1881, 11 mo. 15.

(1169.) Amos Addis Martindell—another son of Mary Hutchinson Addis and Jonathan Warner Martindell, her husband—was born 1857, 3d month 19; married Jennie Fesmier, 1880, 1st month 1. Have a child:

1996. Ada M. Martindell, b. 1881, 2 mo. 24.

(1177.) George Courtney Lingerman—a son of Ann Elizabeth Houpt and Samuel D. Lingerman, her husband—was born 1847, 11th month 28; married 1866, 7th month 2, Martha A. Vansant. Has children:

1997. Clara Lingerman, b. 1868, 8 mo. 22.
1998. Samuel Houpt Lingerman, b. 1870, 7 mo. 22.
1999. Carrie Vansant Lingerman, b. 1872, 11 mo. 15.

(William[6], Martha[5], William[4], Joseph[3], William[2], William[1].)
(1259.) Edward Q. Pool[7]—a son of William C. Pool and Maria Thompson, his wife—was born 1834, 3d month 9; married in 1862, Lizzie Lukens. Their children are:

2000. Kate Pool, b. 1862, d. 1875.
2001. William Pool.
2002. James L. Pool.
2003. Henry Pool.
2004. Maggie Pool.

(1260.) John T. Pool—another son of William C. Pool and Maria Thompson, his wife—was born in Buckingham, Pa.; married Pricilla Smith, 1873, 2nd month 20. Their children are:

2005. Ella J. Pool, b. 1871, 1 mo. 4, d. in infancy.
2006. Joseph S. Pool, b. 1875, 8 mo. 11, d. 7 weeks old.
2007. Emma S. Pool, b. 1876, 11 mo. 10.
2008. Anna Maria Pool, b. 1878, 2 mo. 4.
2009. Frank B. Pool, b. 1880, 5 mo. 16, d. 1881.
2010. Sarah Pool, b. 1882, 7 mo. 12.

WILLIAM CARVER

(1262.) Samuel T. Pool—another son of William C. Pool and Maria Thompson, his wife—was born 1842, 1st month 16; married Helen Beal in 1868. Have children:

2011. Samuel Pool.
2012. Alwyn Pool.
2013. Helen Pool.
2014. Beatrice M. Pool.

(William C.[6], Martha[5], William[4], Joseph[3], William[2], William[1].)
(1265.) Thomas T. Pool[7]—another son of William C. Pool and Maria Thompson, his wife—was born in Buckingham, 1848, 3d month 10; married Jane Eliza Slack, daughter of Albert, in 1870. Have childred:

2015. Albert Pool.
2016. Nellie Darrak Pool.

(Izri[6], Martha[5], William[4], Joseph[3], William[2], William[1].)
(1266.) William Pool[7]—a son of Izri Pool and Evelina Terry, his wife—married Isabella McMillen. Have a child:

2017. Edwin Pool.

(Edward[6], Martha[5], William[4], Joseph[3], William[2], William[1].)
(1271.) Margaret Pool[7]—a daughter of Edward Q. Pool and Mary Thornton, his wife—was born 1842, 7th month 13—married Jacob F. Lefferts, died 1872, 1st month 15. Had one child:

2018. Frank C. Lefferts.

(1272.) Rachel Pool—another daughter of Edward Q. Pool and Mary Thornton, his wife—married William La Rue. Has children:

2019. Mary La Rue.
2020. William La Rue.

(1273.) Almira Pool—another daughter of Edward Q. Pool and Mary Thornton, his wife—married 1875, 11th month 25, Hiram Hellyer. Have one child:

2021. Edward P. Hellyer.

(1274.) Martha Pool—another daughter of Edward Q. Pool and Mary Thornton, his wife—married Albert Slack. Has children:

2022. Edward Slack.
2023. Josiah Slack.
2024. George Slack.

(1275.) Winfield S. Pool—a son of Edward Q. Pool and Mary Thornton, his wife—married Lydia Van Hart. Has children:

2025. Margaret Pool.
2026. John S. Pool.

(John[6], Hannah[5], William[4], Joseph[3], William[2], William[1].)
(1284.) Caroline Kimble[7]—a daughter of John—married Patric Harford—has children:

2027. Laura Harford.
2028. Mary Harford.
2029. Louisa Harford.
2030. Evelina Harford.
2031. Robert Harford.
2032. Charles Harford.

(John[6], Hannah[5], William[4], Joseph[3], William[2], William[1].)
(1288.) Rosella Kimble[7]—another daughter of John Kimble and Catharine King, his wife—was born 1858, 8th month 5; married Frank Groom. Have a child:

2033. ——— Groom.

(John[6], Hannah[5], William[4], Joseph[3], William[2], William[1].)
(1289.) Walter Kimble[7]—another son of John Kimble and Catharine King, his wife—was born 1860, 8th month 6th: married Catharine Coomb. Have a child:

2034. ——— Kimble.

(1292. Hannah Bodine—a daughter of Martha Kimble and John McClure Bodine—was twice married: first, to John Cook in 1852; he died, and in 1879 she married John Morgan. Her children are:

2035. Clara Cook, d.
2036. Jennie Cook.
2037. Edgar Cook.
2038. Lincoln Cook.
2039. William Morgan.
2040. Leonard Morgan.
2041. Louisa Morgan.

(1296.) Ella Bodine—another daughter of Martha Kimble and John McClure Bodine, her husband—married in 1878, Elias Bennett. Children:

2042. Eva Bennett.
2043. Edgar Bennett.

(1298.) William Large—a son of Hannah Kimble and John Large, her husband—married and had four children:

2044. Laura Large.
2045. William Large.
2046. John Large.
2047. ———— Large, a daughter.

(1299.) Louisa Large—a daughter of John Large and Hannah Kimble, his wife—married William Henderson. Have a child:

2048. Hannah Henderson.

(1300.) Elizabeth Large—another daughter of John Large and Hannah Kimble, his wife—was three times married: first, to James Vandegrift; secondly, to William Moreland; and thirdly, to William Henry. Had children:

2049. John Vandegrift.
2050. Lilian Moreland.

(Hannah[6], Hannah[5], William[4], Joseph[3], William[2], William[1].)

(1301.) Mary Ann Large[7]—another daughter of Hannah Kimble and John Large, her husband—married William Moore, died leaving two children:

2051. Hannah Moore.
2052. William Moore.

(1302.) John Blackson—a son of Elizabeth Kimble and Moses Blackson, her husband—married Emma Gallager. Has one child:

2053. Walter Gallager Blackson.

(1305.) Seruch Titus Kimble—a son of Henry Kimble and Mary Titus, his wife—was born in 1849, 4th month 4; married Ada Slack, died at Appleton, Cecil Co., Maryland, on Sunday, 1885, 2nd month 8. Had one child:

2054. Fanny Kimble.

(1306.) John Titus Kimble—another son of Henry Kimble and Mary Titus, his wife—married Teressa Gallager. Had children:

2055. Mary Kimble.
2056. Ida Kimble.
2057. Evelina Kimble.
2058. Henry Kimble.
2059. ———— Kimble, a son.

(1307.) Irvin T. Ruth—a son of Martha P. Carver and Jesse Ruth, her husband—was born in Buckingham, studied law with Hon. George Lear, and was admitted to the Bucks County Bar, 1871, 9th month 11. He died unmarried.

(1314.) George Ruth—a son of Martha P. Carver and Jesse Ruth, her husband—was twice married: first, to Lucretia ———, she died; secondly, to Maggie Wiggins. Had two children by first wife:

2060. Mary Ruth.
2061. George Ruth.

(1315.) Sarah Ruth—a daughter of Martha P. Carver and Jesse Ruth, her husband—was born in Buckingham, married Stephen K. Atkinson, son of Jesse L., in 1877. Have children:

2062. Elener H. Atkinson.
2063. Martha Ruth Atkinson.

Kirk Carver—a son of Stricklin Carver and Asenath White, his wife—married Mary Morgan, 1872, 11th month 30. Have children:

Annie Carver.
George Carver.
William Carver.
Bertha Carver.
Herbert Carver. } See No. (654), Page 114.
Letitia Carver.
Chester Carver.
Ada Carver.

(1438.) Henrietta C. Slack—a daughter of Joseph C. Slack and Elizabeth B. Carver, his wife—was born in Northampton Twp, Bucks Co., Pa., on 5th day, 1858, 4th month 8. She and Doctor Fred Swartzlander of the same Township were married July 18, 1877. They lived in Richborough, Bucks Co., Pa., where he practiced his profession until the summer of 1887, when they moved to Omaha, Nebraska, where they now reside. The following are their children:

2064. Joseph C. Swartzlander, b. 1880, 4 mo. 8, in Bucks Co., Pa.
2065. Louis Swartzlander, b. 1882, 3 mo. 6, in Bucks Co., Pa.
2066. Ann Elizabeth Swartzlander, b. 1883, 9 mo. 21, d. 1885, 1 mo. 10.
2067. Henry C. Swartzlander, b. 1889, 4 mo. 17, in Omaha, Neb.
2068. Friedaricka Swartzlander, b. 1890, 10 mo. 9, in Omaha, Neb.

The doctor and his wife visited Europe before they went to Omaha to live, and also the Yellow Stone Park, and went from Portland, Oregon by stage to San Francisco, Cal.

Louis Swartzlander, their second child, enlisted in the cavalry service and was in the Philippine War for about two years, when he was between 17 and 18 years old.

INDEX

Agnes Carver, 972.
Amos Carver, 90, 146, 366, 1076, 1496.
Adella Carver, 770.
Aaron Carver, 211.
Aden Carver, 362.
Albert W. Carver, 214, 714.
Ada Carver, 1873.
Alfred S. Carver, 219.
Addie C. Carver, 721.
Alfred Carver, 341, 559, 1883.
Alonzo L. Carver, 1074.
Amy Carver, 101, 1024.
Albina Carver, 1037.
Angelina Carver, 109, 327, 702, 754, 930.
Anthony Carver, 58.
Amanda Carver, 234.
Anderson Carver, 1013.
Ann Carver, 50, 102, 106, 133, 143, 202, 326, 677, 692, 697, 1012, 1866.
Anna E. Carver, 1504, 1587, 1951.
Anna Malissa Carver, 583.

Benjamin Carver, 31, 58, 188, 210, 243, 546.
Bertha A. Carver, 15, 16, 1869, 1949.
Beulah Carver, 186, 1078.

Caroline Carver, 200, 374, 551, 1605.
Chapman Carver, 1014.
Charles Carver, 204, 231, 360, 259, 597, 1615, 1063, 1307.
Clemens Carver, 353, 1007.
Chester Carver, 1872.
Cephas Ross Carver, 530.
C. Harrison Carver, 257.
Clara Carver, 684, 751.
Comley Carver, 850.
Cornelius Carver, 77.
Cynthia Carver, 376, 561, 984, 1011.
Cecilia E. Carver, 531.
Derrick H. Carver, 320.

David P. Carver, 48, 126, 177.
Davis W. Carver, 602.
Deborah H. Carver, 178.

Edward B. Carver, 1953.
Edgar Carver, 933.
Edmund P. Carver, 536, 1592.

Eber L. Carver, 534.
Ella L. Carver, 708, 1915.
Ellen Carver, 856, 965, 1042, 1072.
Edwin Carver, 223, 784, 988.
Elmira Carver, 593.
Emma Carver, 599, 701, 722, 931.
Emily Carver, 510, 1016.
Elias Carver, 512, 586.
Ely Carver, 379.
Eliza Carver, 63.
Elizabeth Carver, 11, 17, 26, 109, 128, 156, 256, 331, 363, 458, 478, 506, 511, 527, 964, 776, 785, 1593, 1614, 1912.
Ellicott Carver, 1407.
Edward Carver, 1060.
Ellwood Carver, 1021.
Emmer Carver, 1006, 1463, 1887.
Elmer E. Carver, 1515.
Ermina V. Carver, 1045, 1508.
Enos B. Carver, 1004.
Eva Carver, 1077.
Esther Carver, 59.
Evelina P. Carver, 183.
Eseck H. Carver, 1065.
Eugene Carver, 229.
Euphemia V. Carver, 342.

Frank M. Carver, 174, 203, 935, 1882.
Fannie Carver, 1159.

Garret V. Carver, 78, 343.
George W. Carver, 191, 207, 212, 357, 595, 685, 1039, 1071, 1589, 1867, 1512, 1886.
Grace A. Carver, 1520.

Hannah Carver, 7, 89, 111, 225, 338, 354, 507, 528, 703, 789, 1010.
Henry Carver, 10, 127, 138, 140, 196, 228, 502, 601, 934, 1009, 1040, 1439, 1588.
Major Henry Carver, 51.
Harrison Carver, 218, 1053.
Harriet Carver, 221, 994.
Harry Carver, 664, 709, 1521, 1439, 1588.
Herbert L. Carver, 666, 1820.
Howard Carver, 1069.

Ida V. Carver, 1067.
Isaac Carver, 91, 152, 1038.
Isabella F. Carver, 779.

Izri Carver, 113.
Israel Carver, 1067.
Ida V. Carver, 1067.
Isaac Carver, 91, 152, 1038.

Jacob Carver, 105.
James Carver, 53, 129, 350, 362, 717, 1495.
Jane Carver, 182, 328, 339, 549.
Jannie M. Carver, 1460.
Jessie P. Carver, 62, 148, 253, 367.
Jessie A. Carver, 1514.
Joel Carver, 20, 82, 93, 332.
John Carver, 21, 29, 108, 93, 136, 203, 337, 348, 365, 588, 959, 989, 1005, 1406, 1518, 1948, 1585.
Joseph Carver, 9, 16, 19, 30, 52, 60, 79, 90, 100, 254, 259, 321, 329, 351, 359, 361, 505, 526, 690, 720, 769, 982, 1613, 1495.
Jenkens Ross Carver, 525.
Julia H. Carver, 145, 508.
Johanna Carver, 592, 717.

Kate Carver, 206, 233.
Keziah Carver, 373, 854.
Kirk Carver, 654.

Lama S. Carver, 706, 736.
Lafayette Carver, 1023.
Laura S. Carver, 706, 736.
Letitia E. Carver, 135, 1871, 1057.
Levi Carver, 94, 151, 557, 1594.
Lewis Carver, 553, 258, 1046.
Linda A. Carver, 783.
Loretta Carver, 1018.
Lucinda Carver, 585.
Louisa Carver, 590.
Lizzie Carver, 973, 1513, 1884.
Lettie Carver, 1916.

Margaret Carver, 197, 232, 377.
Maggie R. Carver, 778.
Maria Carver, 208, 987, 1408.
Mahlon Carver, 857.
Marjary Carver, 962.
Martha Carver, 14, 23, 81, 88, 98, 107, 241½, 457, 533, 963, 1506.
Mary Carver, 6, 12, 18, 80, 100, 142, 154, 179, 187, 205, 224, 255, 322, 336, 356, 358, 375, 509, 524, 542, 584, 596, 655, 772, 782, 853, 961, 974, 982.
Miranda Carver, 1043.
Marietta Carver, 1062.
Marshall Carver, 1058.
Milton Carver, 1459.
Mercy Carver, 855.
Mattie B. Carver, 753.
Miller D. Carver, 95.
Miles Carver, 49, 61, 97, 222, 241,

Miranda Carver, 153.
Milton Carver, 1459.
Mitchell Carver, 693.
Modecai Carver, 547.

Nathan C. Carver, 227, 240, 719.
Nellie Carver, 1517.
Nelson Carver, 201.

Oliver Carver, 370.
Orville Ray Carver, 1957.

Pamelia Carver, 132.
Paxson Carver, 220.
Phebe Carver, 99, 215, 226, 1070.
Preston C. Carver, 1604.

Rebecca Carver, 4, 13, 137, 318, 587.
Rachel Carver, 2, 24, 26, 87, 130, 141, 150, 210, 545½, 591, 699, 1950, 1952.
Reading Carver, 1055.
Richard M. Carver, 1054.
Robert W. Carver, 695, 960.
Ross Carver, 700.
Roxanna Carver, 773, 1073.
Ruth Carver, 22.

Samuel Carver, 125, 333, 349, 550, 560, 737, 1020, 1505.
Sarah Carver, 1, 54, 56, 134, 175, 319, 480, 504, 548, 589, 969, 1052, 1041, 1066, 1505. 1020
Smith Carver, 242, 330.
Sophia Carver, 562.
Stephen Carver, 155, 185, 213, 698, 1591.
Strickland Carver, 180.
Susanna O. Carver, 723.

T. Ellwood Carver, 189.
Terissa Carver, 718.
Theodore Carver, 184, 665.
Thomas Carver, 28, 131, 139, 198, 501, 556, 1009, 1059.
Titus Carver, 1911.

Warren Carver, 1022.
Watson Carver, 1056, 1495.
Walton S. Carver, 535, 281, 1008, 1015.
Winfield Carver, 1061.
Wilhelmina Carver, 715, 716.
Willets Carver, 199, 1590.
Wilson Carver, 371, 777, 252.
William Carver, 1, 3, 8, 15, 25, 57, 112, 147, 176, 195, 217, 251, 334, 352, 456, 502, 555, 594, 691, 771, 775, 852, 932, 966, 967, 1868, 1586, 1507, 1455, 1453, 1616, 1044.

Yardley Carver, 369.

John Carver Addis, 397.
Ellen Addis, 398.
Isaac Clarkson Addis, 399.
Eliza Ann Addis, 400.
Mary Hutchinson Addis, 401.
John Clarkson Addis, 1149.
Amos Addis, 1150.
Snowden Addis, 1151.
George F. Addis, 1152.
Jonathan W. Addis, 1153.
Robert Addis, 1154.
Herman S. Addis, 1155.
Amy Addis, 1158.
Anna Addis, 1159.
Howard Addis, 1160.
Romand L. Addis, 1991.
Leonard Payne Addis, 1992.
Lavinia Gertrude Addis, 1993.

Harvey Abbott, 1987.
Anna L. Abbott, 1988.

Oliver C. Allen, 537.
Alfred E. Allen, 538.
Caroline W. Allen, 539.
Joseph C. Allen, 540.
Hannah A. Allen, 541.
Mary B. Allen, 542.
Martha C. Allen, 543.
Elizabeth C. Allen, 544.
Rachel S. Allen, 545.
Samuel Allen, 1464.
William Allen, 1465.
Harry Allen, 1466.
Walter Allen, 1470.
Howard Allen, 1471.
William Allen, 1472.
Salley M. Armatage, 920.

Lizzie Atchley, 1946.
Ella Atchley, 1947.

Georgiene Atkinson, 747.
William S. Atkinson, 748.
Stephen R. Atkinson, 749.
Sallie M. Atkinson, 750.
Elener H. Atkinson, 1887.
Martha Ruth Atkinson, 1888.

Elener H. Atkinson, 2062.
Martha Ruth Atkinson, 2063.
Mary Ann Beans, 414.
Sarah T. Beans, 415.
Amanda Beans, 416.
Eliza L. Beans, 417.
Anna Mary Beans, 975.
Carrie Beans, 976.

Annie E. Beans, 977.
Mary C. Beans, 978.
Alice Beans, 979.

Elizabeth W. Barber, 1362.
Elliston P. Barber, 1363.
Mary Arrilla Barber, 1363½.
Amos Walker Barber, 1364.
Meta Bell Barber, 1365.
Edward Shaw Barber, 1386.

Ella Barton, 731.
Edward Barton, 732.
James Barton, 733.
Emma Barton, 733½.
William Barton, 734.

Edward Baily, 1030.
Randolph Kirk Betts, 304.
Mary Kirk Betts, 305.
Sarah Ann Betts, 306.
Letitia Anderson Betts, 307.
Simpson Carey Betts, 308.
Martha M. Betts, 308½.
S. Lorenzo Betts, 909.
Lorenzo Betts, 1088.

Henry Bennet, 1874.
——— Bennet, 1075.
Stephen Bennet, 1876.
Miles Bennet, 1877.
Daughter Bennet, 1878.
Eva Bennet, 2042.
Edgar Bennet, 2043.

Emily Adell Bellemere, 1638.
Henry Kirk Bellemere, 1639.
John Francis Bellemere, 1640.
Wm. H. Bellemere, 1641.
Chas. H. M. Bellemere, 1642.

Jonathan W. Black, 1359.
Lorenzo D. Black, 1360.
Edward Black, 1361.
Jesse Black, 609.
Julia Black, 610.
Sarah G. Black, 611.
Henry Black, 612.
Benjamin Black, 613.
Kirk Black, 614.
Elizabeth F. Black, 615.
Rebecca J. Black, 616.
Eli Black, 617.
Mary Black, 618.
Alonzo Black, 1542.
Herman J. Black, 1543.

Melissa M. Black, 1544.
Wm. H. Black, 1545.
E. Anna Black, 1546.
Jesse M. Black, 1547.
Abraham Black, 1548.
Sarah A. Black, 1549.
Arian Black, 1550.
John W. Black, 1551.
Harriet Ella Black, 1552.
Anna M. Black, 1553.
Caroline P. Black, 1554.
Pennington Black, 1555, 1568.
Estella Black, 1556.
Anna Estella Black, 1557.
Ada D. Black, 1558.
Miller R. Black, 1559.
Louis Black, 1560.
Joseph Black, 1561.
Bertha Black, 1562.
Oliver Black, 1563.
Hannah Black, 1567.
Franklin Black, 1569.
Elizabeth L. Black, 1570.
Carey Black, 1571.
Charles Black, 1572.
Della Black, 1573.
Wm. S. Black, 1631.
Horace W. Black, 1632.
Kirk Black, 1633.
Ann Elizabeth Black, 1634.
William Black, 1637.
Abraham Black, 1643.
Sarah Ann Black, 1644.
Henry Black, 1645.
Benjamin Black, 1646.

Hannah Ellen Blaker, 767.
Wm. Winfield Blaker, 768.
Henry D. Bloom, 1968.
John Blackston, 1202.
Hannah Blackson, 1203.
Charles M. Blaker, 250.
Hannah Blaker, 767.
Angelina C. Blaker, 766.
William Winfield Blaker, 768.

Hannah Bodine, 1292.
David Bodine, 1293.
Martha Bodine, 1294.
Elizabeth Bodine, 1295.
Ella Bodine, 1296.
Anna Bodine, 1297.

Joseph Carver Booth, 1409.
Julia Arabella Booth, 1410.
Mary Elizabeth Booth, 1411.
Wm. Hoyle Booth, 1412.

Emily Jane Booth, 1413.
Edward Boyer, 638.
Susan J. Brown, 1935.
Wm. L. Brown, 1936.
Howard C. Brown, 1937.

Sarah Bradshaw, 64.
Wm. Bradshaw, 65.
Sidney Bradshaw, 66.
David Bradshaw, 67.
Ruth Bradshaw, 68.
James Bradshaw, 69.
Elizabeth Bradshaw, 70.
Phebe Bradshaw, 264.
Isaac Bradshaw, 265.
David Heston Bradshaw, 270.
Joseph Bradshaw, 271.
Lewis W. Bradshaw, 272.
Seraphina Bradshaw, 273.
Rebecca Bradshaw, 274.
Anna M. Bradshaw, 275.
Mary Elizabeth Bradshaw, 276.
Malicent Bradshaw, 807.
Ellen Bradshaw, 808.
Henry Bradshaw, 809.
Malicent Bradshaw, 810.
Sallie Bradshaw, 811.

Mary Anna Broadhurst, 514.
Samuel Broadhurst, 515.
Caroline L. Broadhurst, 516.
Joseph J. Broadhurst, 1442.
Ann M. Broadhurst, 1443.
Horace G. Broadhurst, 1444.

Anna Frances Buckman, 632.
S. Harrold Buckman, 634.
Caroline L. Buckman, 633.
Malcolm A. Buckman, 927.
Thomas W. Bye, 323.

Joseph C. Bye, 324.
Allen R. Bye, 325.
John Hart Bye, 942.
Sarah V. Bye, 943.
Anna R. Bye, 945.
Mary V. Bye, 944.
Franklin P. Bye, 946.
Lorenzo Seaman Bye, 947.
Josephine Bye, 949.
Pleasant Bye, 948.
Allen Bye, Jr., 950.
Nathan F. Bye, 951.
Elizabeth F. Bye, 952.

Rachel Ann Caffee, 1497.
Ralph A. Caffee, 1498.
Mordecai Caffee, 1499.

Mary Eliza Caffee, 1500.
Theodore B. Caffee, 1501.
Laura Matilda Caffee, 1502.
Sarah Jane Caffee, 1503.

Jane Elizabeth Carey, 1510.
Mary Martha Carey, 1509.
Georgiana Carey, 1511.

Rebecca Carr, 503.
J. Watson Case, 493.
Sarah K. Case, 494.
William E. Case, 495.
Caroline B. Case, 496.
Henry C. Case, 497.
Rebecca C. Case, 498.
Elizabeth F. Case, 499.
Samuel C. Case, 500.
Harriet S. Case, 1388.
Letitia Case, 1389.
Sarah E. Case, 1390.
Edward G. Case, 1391.
Wm. Schuyler Case, 1393.
Philip A. Case, 1394.
Anna Parsons Case, 1395.
Mary W. Case, 1397.
Caroline S. Case, 1398.
Florence N. Case, 1399.
Samuel S. Case, 1400.
Horace E. Case, 1401.
Nettie DuBois Case, 1403.
Henry Carver Case, 1404.
Ella Black Case, 1405.

Benjamin Casner, 1478.
Samuel Casner, 1479.
Amos Casner, 1480.
Alexander H. Casner, 1481.
John Casner, 1482.
Elizabeth Casner, 1483.
Enos Casner, 1484.
Clinton Casner, 1485.
Caroline Casner, 1486.
Wm. Casner, 1487.
Annie Casner, 1488.

John Richard Clemens, 1146.
Mary Agnes Clemens, 1147.
Anna A. Clemens, 1148.

James Chew, 1222.
Benjamin Chew, 1223.
Kate Chew, 1224.

William Church, 1247.
Watson Church, 1248.
Mary Church, 1249.
Harry Church, 1250.
Annie Church, 1251.

Stephen K. Cooper, 898.
Sarah E. Corson, 918.
Edward Corson, 919.

Mary Conover, 1889.
Florence Clemens, 1990.

John Chittick, 1913.
——— Chittick, 1914.

Clara Cook, 2035.
Jennie Cook, 2036.
Edger Cook, 2037.
Lincoln Cook, 2038.
Emma Ann Cornell, 936.
Mary Jane Cornell, 937.
Albert Cornell, 938.
Henry Cornell, 939.
William Cornell, 940.
Margaret Cornell, 941.
Franklin Cornell, 942.
Jane Eliza Cornell, 1896.

Sarah E. Corson, 918.
Edward Corson, 919.
Audery Cosner, 1031.
Mary H. Cosner, 1032.
Jesse Cosner, 1033.
Horatio M. Cosner, 1034.
Thomas Cosner, 1035.
Joseph Cosner, 1036.

George H. Davis, 710.
Edward Davis, 711.
Jos. A. Davis, 712.
Henrietta Davis, 713.
Mary Oldden Davis, 1323.

Evelina Doan, 293.
John K. Doan, 294.
Eleazer Doan, 295.
Amos Doan, 296.
Wm. K. Doan, 297.
Benjamin C. Doan, 298.
Stephen K. Doan, 299.
Theodore J. Doan, 300.
Mary Doan, 301.
Sarah S. Doan, 302.
Miranda K. Doan, 303.
Annie K. Doan, 667.
Augustus W. Doan, 877.
Edward C. Doan, 878.
Eleazer T. Doan, 879.
B. Frank Doan, 880.
Henry Doan, 881.
Benjamin E. Doan, 882.
Hannah K. Doan, 883.
Sarah Doan, 884.
Martha Doan, 885.
Miranda Doan, 886.

Horace Doan, 887.
Warran Doan, 888.
Josephine Doan, 889.
Flora Doan, 890.
Charles Doan, 891.
Benjamin Doan, 892.
Annie K. Doan, 893.
Theodore J. Doan, 894.
Miranda Doan, 895.
Adella Doan, 896.
Clara M. Doan, 897.

Ann Drake, 1929.
Adolphus Drake, 1930.
Harry Drake, 1931.
Mary Drake, 1932.

Charles Eastburn, 517.
Henry C. Eastburn, 518.
Joseph C. Eastburn, 519.
Edward Eastburn, 520.
Hannah C. Eastburn, 521.
Rachel Eastburn, 522.
George L. Eastburn, 899.
Isabella Eastburn, 900.
Rebecca Gillingham Elton, 459.
Elizabeth Gillingham Elton, 460.
Josephine Gillingham Elton, 461.
Hugh B. Eastburn, 1323.
Fanney C. Eastburn, 1324.

Franklin B. Ellis, 812.
J. Watson Ellis, 813.
Charles W. Ellis, 814.
Albro L. Ellis, 815.
Bessie Ellis, 816.

Hugh B. Ely, 117.
Charles Ely, 118.
Joseph Ely, 119.
Wm. C. Ely, 120.
Alfred Ely, 121.
Henry C. Ely, 122.
Alfred Ely, 123.
Joseph Ely, 124.
Achsah M. Ely, 462.

Mary Anna Ely, 463.
Francenia Ely, 464.
Joseph Oldden Ely, 465.
Alfred Ely, 466.
Charles Bennington Ely, 467.
Wm. Penn Ely, 468.
Catharine O. Ely, 469.
Hugh B. Ely, 470.
Rachel S. Ely, 471.

Elizabeth C. Ely, 472.
Holmes D. Ely, 473.
Richard Watson Ely, 474.
Sarah Y. Ely, 475.
Thomas H. Ely, 476.
Wm. C. Ely, Jr., 477.
Mary Anna Ely, 901.
Watson Ely, 902.
Kizzie Ely, 903.
Hannah Ely, 904.
Isaac Ely, 905.
Emma Ely, 906.
George Franklin Ely, 1190.
Anna Mary Ely, 1191.
Walter Ely, 1192.
Elmer Ellsworth Ely, 1193.
Alfred Ely, 1325.
Jane K. Ely, 1326.
Hugh B. Ely, 1327.
Wm. Penn Ely, 1328.
Walter Ely, 1329.
Lettie Ely, 1330.
Sarah Ely, 1331.
Catharine H. Ely, 1332.
Rachel Ely, 1333.
Mary D. Ely, 1334.
Hugh B. Ely, 1335.
Grace Holmes Ely, 1336.
Lilian Stead Ely, 1353.
William Parker Ely, 1354.
John Anderson Ely, 1355.
Alfred Thomas Ely, 1356.
Mary Anna Eastburn Ely, 1357.
Holmes Davis Ely, 1358.
Able Ely, 1473.
William Ely, 1474.
Mary Ely, 1475.

William Erwin, 1185.
John Erwin, 1186.
George Erwin, 1187.
Gideon Erwin, 1188.

Martha Everett, 953.
Alice Everett, 954.
Randolph Everett, 955.
Elmira Ewer, 1919.
Nellie Erving, 380.

John Howard Evans, 1132.
Henry L. Evans, 1133.
Ann Evans, 1134.
Augusta Evans, 1135.
Agnes Evans, 1136.
Emily Ann Evans, 1137.
J. Newton Evans, 1138.
Heston Evans, 1139.

Ida Jane Evans, 1579.
Wilson C. Evans, 1635.
Mary Emma Evans, 1636.
Joseph Samuel Evans, 1989.

Caleb Firman, 1647.
Eli Firman, 1648.
Sarah Firman, 1649.
Letitia Firman, 1650.

Jane Eliza Coe Fly, 573.
Wilamina Maria Fly, 574.
Levina Fly, 575.
Isaac Otis Fly, 576.
Sarah Ann Fly, 577.
Martha B. Fly, 578.
Caroline Fly, 579.
Mary H. Fly, 580.
Elizabeth Ann Fly, 581.
Joseph Carver Fly, 582.
Rachel C. Fly, 583.
Howard W. Flack, 1366.
John Dyer Flack, 1367.

Mahlon Gilbert, 384.
George W. Gilbert, 385.
Lydia Ann Gilbert, 386.
Jonathan Gilbert, 387.
David Gilbert, 388.
John Gilbert, 389.
Rebecca Gilbert, 390.
Howard Gilbert, 391.
Asa Comley Gilbert, 392.
Agnes C. Gilbert, 393.
Matilda Gilbert, 1115.
Evelina Gilbert, 1116.
Theodore Gilbert, 1117.
George Gilbert, 1118.
Daniel Gilbert, 1119.
Elwood Gilbert, 1120.
Harriet Gilbert, 1121.
Mary Gilbert, 1122.
Phoebe Gilbert, 1123.
Elizabeth Gilbert, 1124.
Ann M. Gilbert, 1131.
Edward M. Gilbert, 1130.
Howard Gilbert, 1140.
Nina M. Gilbert, 1141.
Emma Jane Gilbert, 1142.
Florence O. Gilbert, 1143.
Bessie Mary Gilbert, 1144.
John N. Gilbert, 1145.
Theodore Gilbert, 1969.
Walter Gilbert, 1972.
Annie Gilbert, 1973.
Ida Gilbert, 1974.
Nellie Gilbert, 1984.

Maggie Gilbert, 1985.
Wm. Gilbert, 1986.
Rebecca H. Gilpin, 630.
George Gilpin, 631.
Anna Gilpin, 1665.
Henry Gunning, 726.
Alexander Gunning, 727.

Rachel H. Gillingham, 162.
Samuel H. Gillingham, 163.
Mary Ann Gillingham, 164.
Anna Gillingham, 165.
Emmaline L. Gillingham, 166.
Elizabeth Gillingham, 167.
Rebecca Gillingham, 168.
Josephine Gillingham, 169.
Joseph H. Gillingham, 170.
Catharine O. Gillingham, 171.
Frances Gillingham, 172.
Caroline Gillingham, 173.
Fanney Gillingham, 626.
Joseph E. Gillingham, 627.
Lewis H. Gillingham, 628.
Frank C. Gillingham, 629.
William Gillingham, 1863.
Hattie Gillingham, 1864.
Alice J. Green, 787.
———— Groom, 2033.

Mary Ann Beans Goentner, 1202.
Martha Goentner, 1203.
Maria Amanda Goentner, 1204.
Wm. Krider Goentner, 1205.
John Beans Goentner, 1206.
Charles Terry Goentner, 1207.
Mannie Eliza Goentner, 1208.
Sarah Wilhelmina Goentner, 1209.
Wm. Krider Goentner, 1210.
Katharina Goentner, 1211.
Martha Ella Goentner, 1212.
Angelina Goentner, 1213.

Joseph Haines, 404.
Ann Eliza Haines, 405.
Mary F. Hall, 1161.
Amy M. Hall, 1162.
Sallie G. Hall, 1163.
Elizabeth Hall, 1164.
Albert J. Hall, 1165.
Emma Hall, 1236.
Ruth Hall, 1237.

Laura Harford, 2027.
Mary Harford, 2028.
Louisa Harford, 2029.
Evelina Harford, 2030.
Robert Harford, 2031.
Charles Harford, 2032.

Hannah Henderson, 2048.
Rachel Harrold, 33.
David Harrold, 32.
Charles Harrold, 157.
Alfred Harrold, 158.
William Harrold, 159.
Soland Harrold, 160.
Caroline Harrold, 161.
Ralph Harrold, 1653.
Bertha Harrold, 1654.
Annie Harrold, 1655.
Marsella Harrold, 619.
Minnie Harrold, 620.
Oliver Harrold, 620½.
Alfred Harrold, 621.
Maria Harrold, 622.
Emma Harrold, 623.
Annie Harrold, 624.
Seymore Harrold, 625.

Harrison Harvey, 870.
Wm. D. Harvey, 871.
Martha Harvey, 872.
Kinsey Harvey, 874.
Sarah Jane Harvey, 873.
Theodore Harvey, 875.
David Harvey, 876.
Mary Hayes, 1476.
Charles Hayes, 1477.
Marietta Heath, 696.
Edward Hellyer, 2021.

John Hegburn, 1938,
Lilian B. Hegburn, 1939.
Minnie Hegburn, 1940.
Frank Helweg, 1402.
Joseph C. Hibbs, 956.
Sarah Ann Hibbs, 957.
Hannah Hibbs, 958.
Lizzie Hibbs, 1890.
Mary Jane Hibbs, 1891.
George Hibbs, 1892.
Ann Hibbs, 1893.
William Hibbs, 1894.
Benjamin Hibbs, 1895.

Joel Hobensack, 344.
John Hobensack, 345, 996.
George Hobensack, 346.
Ann Hobensack, 347, 1000.
James B. Hobensack, 998.
Emma R. Hobensack, 999.
Ella Hobensack, 1001.
Arcurious Hubbard, 1606.
Elizabeth Hubbard, 1607.
William H. Hubbard, 1608.
William Huber, 1283.

John Huey, 603.
Caroline Huey, 1619.
William Huey, 1626.
Jacob Houpt, 1176.
Robert L. Houpt, 404.
Ann Eliza Houpt, 405.

Claud Johnson, 1627.
Burley Johnson, 1629.
Charles N. Johnson, 1623.
Caroline Johnson, 607.
Flora Johnson, 1626.
Edward Johnson, 604.
George W. Johnson, 605.
Laura Johnson, 1621.
Phebe Johnson, 608, 1622.
Mary L. Johnson, 1630.
Orville C. Johnson, 1628.
William E. Johnson, 606, 1624.
Rebecca C. Johnson, 1396.
Victoria H. Johnson, 1625.

Wm. Kirk, 71.
Sarah Kirk, 72.
Mary Kirk, 73.
John Kirk, 74.
Isaac C. Kirk, 75.
Stephen Kirk, 76.
Rebecca Kirk, 284.
Spencer W. Kirk, 285.
Stephen Smith Kirk, 286, 312.
John M. Kirk, 287.
W. Mitchel Kirk, 288.
Albert Kirk, 289.
Nelson Kirk, 290.
Charles Kirk, 291.
Mary Ellen Kirk, 292.
John Wilson Kirk, 309.
Jos. Comley Kirk, 310.
Thomas Harvey Kirk, 311.
Watson W. Kirk, 313.
Maria L. Kirk, 314.
Mary Jane Kirk, 315.
Rachel Kirk, 316.
Anna L. Kirk, 317.
Lorenzo Kirk, 857.
Ella Kirk, 358.
John T. Kirk, 659.
Emma Kirk, 860.
Pierson Kirk, 861.
Edwin J. Kirk, 862.
Johnson Kirk, 863.
Wm. John Kirk, 864.
Mary C. Kirk, 665.
Lindora Kirk, 866, 1101.
Allen Kirk, 867.
Stephen Kirk, 868, 1103.

Theodore Kirk, 869½.
Chapman Kirk, 907.
Edward Kirk, 908.
Franklin Kirk, 910.
Elvina Kirk, 911.
Walter Kirk, 912.
Elmer Kirk, 913.
Mary Kirk, 914, 1029, 1100.
Rachel Kirk, 915.
Clinton Kirk, 917.
Samuel Kirk, 1025.
Wm. Kirk, 1026, 1099.
Margaret Kirk, 1027.
John Kirk, 1028.
Allen Kirk, 1102.
Ella Kirk, 1920.
Benjamin Kirk, 1921.

Dorrie Kirk, 1922.
Anna Kirk, 1924.
Abbot Kirk, 1925.
Wm. Kirk, 1926.
Mary Kirk, 1927.

John Kimble, Jr., 450.
Martha Kimble, 451.
Hannah Kimble, 452.
Elizabeth Kimble, 453.
George Washington Kimble, 454.
Henry H. Kimble, 455.
———— Kimble, 2034.
Fannie Kimble, 2054.
Mary Kimble, 2055.
Ida Kimble, 2056.
Evelina Kimble, 2057.
Henry Kimble, 2058.
———— Kimble, a son, 2059.
Caroline Kimble, 1284.
Enos Kimble, 1285.
Wm. Kimble, 1286.
Rosella Kimble, 1288.
Lewis Kimble, 1287.
Walter Kimble, 1289.
Mary Kimble, 1290.
Evan Kimble, 1291.
Oscar Kimble, 1304.
Seruch Titus Kimble, 1305.
John Kimble, 1306.

Wm. H. Kibble, 1419.
Ada Gray Kibble, 1420.
Ada F. Kibbee, 1657.
Lucy E. Kibbee, 1658.
Samuel H. Kibbee, 1659.
Henry C. Kibbee, 1660.
Eleanor P. Kibbee, 1661.
Fanny L. Kibbee, 1662.

Fred Kopler, 730.
Thomas Clark King, 1276.
Amos Addis Krusen, 1156.
Helen Krusen, 1157.

Dwight C. Laurance, 823.
David Edison Laurance, 824.
Anna M. Laurance, 825.
Edith Laurance, 826.
Maggie Laurance, 827.
Matilda Lambert, 1079.
William Lambert, 1080.
Abigail Lambert, 1081.
Mary C. Lambert, 1082.
Lucretia Lambert, 1083.
Margery Lambert, 1084.

Frank Large, 1234.
Clayton Large, 1235.
William Large, 1298, 1298.
Louisa Large, 1299.
Elizabeth Large, 1300.
Mary Anna Large, 1301.
Laura Large, 2044.
William Large, 2045.
John Large, 2046.
———— Large, daughter, 2047.

Flora Z. Lewis, 644.
Ida M. Lewis, 645.
Howard A. Lewis, 646.
Fannie S. Lewis, 647.
Evan T. Lewis, 648.
Sallie W. Lewis, 649.
Franklin H. Lewis, 650.
Daniel Lewis, 1970.
Harry Lewis, 1971.

John Linburg, 280, 834.
Benjamin M. Linburg, 281.
Ruth Ann Linburg, 282.
Howard Linburg, 283.
Gertrude Linburg, 835.
Mary Linburg, 836.
Florence Linburg, 837.
Edna Linburg, 838.
Theodore Linburg, 839.

George Courtney Lingerman, 1177.
Richard C. Lingerman, 1178.
Mary Ellen Lingerman, 1179.
Harry A. Lingerman, 1180.
Anna C. Lingerman, 1181.
Jennie Ward Lingerman, 1182.
Clara Lingerman, 1997.
Samuel H. Lingerman, 1998.
Carrie Vansant Lingerman, 1999.
Walter Lineaweaver, 1456.

Etta Leatherman, 1489.
Zachary Leatherman, 1490.
Charles P. Leatherman, 1491.
R. Lizzie Leatherman, 1492.
Della P. Leatherman, 1493.
Anna B. Leatherman, 1494.

Holmes E. La Rue, 1345.
George G. La Rue, 1346.
Theodore B. La Rue, 1347.
Martha S. La Rue, 1348.
Silas Palissy La Rue, 1349.
Elizabeth Ely La Rue, 1350.
Warran Jacquese Le Rue, 1351.
James Malcom La Rue, 1352.
Mary La Rue, 2019.
William La Rue, 2020.
William Wallace Lee, 926.

Wilson Lippincott, 828.
Watson Lippincott, 829.
Ellsworth Lippincott, 831.
Anna B. Lippincott, 830.
Martin Lippincott, 832.
Ruth Lippincott, 833.
Francis Buck Livezey, 1316.
Thos. Elton Livezey, 1317.
Paxson Elton Livezey, 1318.
George Gillingham Livezey, 1319.
Elizabeth Elton Livezey, 1320.
Josephine Livezey, 1321.

John Lloyd, 340.
E. Morris Lloyd, 958.
Henry C. Lloyd, 986.
Henry A. Lloyd, 1904.
James D. Lloyd, 1905.
Henry A. Lloyd, 1906.
John M. Lloyd, 1907.
Enos Morris Lloyd, 1908.
Wm. Y. Lloyd, 1909.
Amanda F. Lloyd, 1910.

Frank C. Lefferts, 2018.
James McDowell, 192.
Napoleon McDowell, 193.
Martha McDowell, 194.
Eliza Ann McDowell, 224.
Hannah McDowell, 245, 673, 761.
George McDowell, 246, 670, 759.
Joseph McDowell, 247.
William McDowell, 248, 763, 757.
Robert McDowell, 249.
Henry McDowell, 671.
Caroline McDowell, 672.
A. Caroline McDowell, 755.
Esther McDowell, 756.
Kinsey McDowell, 758.

Ann McDowell, 760.
Clarissa McDowell, 762.
Jennie McDowell, 764.
Letitia McDowell, 765.
Ida E. McLean, 1617.
Harry C. McLean, 1618.
Elizabeth S. McNelly, 1966.
Catharine McNally, 1967.

Ruth Ann Meredith, 277.
Anna Maria Meredith, 278.
Watson Meredith, 279.
Thomas H. Martindell, 1166.
Miles M. Martindell, 1167.
Annie Addis Martindell, 1168.
Amos Addis Martindell, 1169.
Edwin W. Martindell, 1170.
Isaiah M. Martindell, 1171.
Benjamin C. Martindell, 1172.
Jonathan W. Martindell, 1173.
Mary M. Martindell, 1174.
Emma J. Martindell, 1175.
Harry E. Martendale, 1994.
Bertha A. Martendale, 1995.
Ada Martendale, 1996.
Martha C. Messimer, 1452.
Clara Middleton, 686.
Henrietta Middleton, 687.
Willis Middleton, 688.
Mervill Middleton, 689.
Elmira C. Milnor, 1609.

Frank Miller, 651.
Wm. E. Miller, 652.
Carrie Miller, 653.
Caroline Miller, 674.
Adaline Miller, 675.
Kate Miller, 676.
Nelson Miller, 1954.
Adin Miller, 1955.
Walter Miller, 1956.

Lilian Moreland, 2050.
William Morgan, 2039.
Leonard Morgan, 2040.
Louisa Morgan, 2041.
———— Morgan, son, 1881.
Hannah Moore, 2051.
William Moore, 2052.

Julia Ann Nicholson, 1421.
Wm. Adison Nicholson, 1422.
Mary Emma Nicholson, 1423.
Eva Virginia Nicholson, 1424.
Elizabeth B. Nicholson, 1425.
Sarah Jane Nicholson, 1426.
Giles Oldden, 114.

Catharine Oldden, 115.
Rachel Oldden, 116.

Minerva S. Paist, 266.
D. Bradshaw Paist, 267.
Eliza A. Paist, 269.
J. Monroe Paist, 268.
Josephine Paist, 793.
Samueline Paist, 794.
Jonathan T. Paist, 795.
Sarah E. Paist, 796, 804.
Mary A. Paist, 797, 805.
Charles E. Paist, 798.
Edward H. Paist, 799.
Monroe B. Paist, 800.
Harvey S. Paist, 801.
Alice M. Paist, 802.
Andrew C. Paist, 803.
James H. Paist, 806.

Helen M. Paxson, 1440.
Carrie P. Paxson, 1441.
Robert Beans Phillips, 1899.
John L. Pearson, 840.
Clayton Pearson, 841.
Sallie Pearson, 842.
Filmore Pearson, 843.
Mary Emma Pearson, 844.
Morris Pearson, 845.
Anna Pearson, 846.
Watson Linburg Pearson, 847.
Maggie Pearson, 849.
A. Curtin Pearson, 848.
John Price Pearson, 1238.
William Pearson, 1239.

Esther Peters, 1933.
Martha Peters, 1934.
Robert Beans Phillips, 1899.
Mary Pool, 1256.
Hugh Thompson Pool, 1257.
Martha Pool, 1258.
Edward Pool, 1259.
John T. Pool, 1260.
William Pool, 1261, 1266.
Samuel T. Pool, 1262.
Anna Elizabeth Pool, 1263.
George C. Pool, 1264.
Howard T. Pool, 1265.
Rachel Margaret Pool, 1267.
Catharine Pool, 1268.
Elizabeth Pool, 1269.
Martha Pool, 1270, 1274.
Margaret Pool, 1271.
Rachel Pool, 1272.
Almira Pool, 1273.
Winfield S. Pool, 1275.

Kate Pool, 2000.
William Pool, 2001.
James L. Pool, 2002.
Harry Pool, 2003.
Maggie Pool, 2004.
Ella J. Pool, 2005.
Joseph S. Pool, 2006.
Emma S. Pool, 2007.
Anna Maria Pool, 2008.
Frank B. Pool, 2009.
Sarah Pool, 2010.
Samuel Pool, 2011.
Alwyn Pool, 2012.
Helen Pool, 2013.
Beatrice Pool, 2014.
William C. Pool, 441.
Izri Pool, 442.
Edward Q. Pool, 443.
Thomas Pool, 444.
Martha Pool, 445.
Albert Pool, 2015.
Nellie Darrak Pool, 2016.
Edwin Pool, 2017.
Margaret Pool, 2025.
John S. Pool, 2026.

John Price, 1240.
Esther Price, 1241.
Harry Price, 1242.
Valentine Price, 1243.
Edward Price, 1244.
Ellen Price, 1245.
Oliver Price, 1246.
Sidney Price, 1252.
Samuel G. Price, 1253.
Edwin Price, 1254.
Mary Price, 1255.
Charles M. Price, 433.
Kirk J. Price, 434.
Stephen K. Price, 435.
Sarah Price, 436.
Smith Price, 437.
Preston Price, 438.
Hannah Price, 439.
John Price, 440.

Mary Ellen Reynolds, 663.
George Rhodes, 1002.
Joseph Rhodes, 1003.
Samuel K. Radcliff, 1923.
Luisa Reading, 1582.
William Reading, 1583.
Anna Mary Reading, 1584.
———— Ramsey, 1975.
Emma A. Rice, 1521½.
Addie A. Rice, 1522.
Mary E. Rice, 1523.

George E. Rice, 1524.
Theressa Rice, 1525.

Hugh B. Romine, 1337.
Jessie E. Romine, 1338.
Lydia D. E. Romine, 1339.
Joseph E. Romine, 1340.
Nellie E. Romine, 1341.
Ruth Hull Romine, 1342.
William C. Ely Romine, 1343.
Cora Kate Romine, 1343¼.
Carrie Beegle Romine, 1343½.
Robert Talpot Romine, 1344.

Annie Rose, 1468.
Lizzie Rose, 1469.
Thomas C. Roach, 1427.
James Franklin Roach, 1428.
Ella Lucinda Roach, 1429.
William Harvey Roach, 1430.
Joseph Ruth Roach, 1431.
Albert Clifton Roach, 1432.
Fred Sherman Roach, 1433.
Clarence Franklin Roach, 1434.
Clara Tamson Roach, 1435.
George Foegal Roach, 1436.
Eava Virginia Roach, 1437.

Ann Rebecca Robinson, 1368.
D. Clinton Robinson, 1369.
Wm. Henry Robinson, 1370.
William Ruth, 1308.
Helen Ruth, 1309.
Josephine Ruth, 1310.
Evan Ruth, 1311.
Adam Ruth, 1312.
Edgar Ruth, 1313.
George Ruth, 2061.
Sallie Ruth, 1315.
Mary Ruth, 2060.
George Ruth, 1314.

Wilhelmina Scott, 729.
George W. Scott, 817.
William Scott, 818.
Edward B. Scott, 819.
David Heston Scott, 820.
S. Milton Scott, 821.
Lizzie S. Scott, 822.
Victoria R. Scott, 1372.
Winfield Scott, 1371.
Anna Permelia Scott, 1373.
Thomas B. Scott, 1374.
Joseph N. Scott, 1375.
Bella R. Scott, 1376.

William Shaw, 635.
Allen Shaw, 636.
Daughter Shaw, 637.
Henrietta Shaw, 678.

Phebe Shaw, 679.
Caroline Shaw, 680.
Anna Shaw, 681.
James M. Shaw, 682.
Alfred Shaw, 489.
Anna Shaw, 490.
John Wilson Shaw, 492.
Marietta Shaw, 491.
Mary Shaw, 1884.
Alfred Shaw, Jr., 1385.
Ettie Prior Shaw, 1387.

Henrietta Slack, 1438.
Edward Slack, 2022.
Josiah Slack, 2023.
George Slack, 2024.
Henrietta Swartzlander, 1438.
Joseph C. Swartzlander, 2064.
Louis Swartzlander, 2065.
Ann Elizabeth Swartzlander, 2066.
Henry C. Swartzlander, 2067.
Friedaricka C. Swartzlander, 2068.

Nellie Stradling, 743.
Anna Stradling, 744.
Smith Stradling, 235.
Mary Stradling, 236.
Miles Stradling, 238.
Hutchinson Stradling, 237.
Martha B. Stradling, 239.
Rachel Stradling, 745.
Elizabeth Stradling, 746.

Isabella Short, 401½.
William Short, 402.
John Short, 403.
Rachel Smith, 523.
Henry Q. Smith, 970.
Lewis Smith, 971.
Martha Smith, 980.
William Smith, 981, 1898.
Carl Smith, 1610.
Elizabeth Smith, 1611.
Elma Smith, 1897.
Hannah Smith, 1903.

Walter Sickel, 740.
Harry Sickel, 742.
Catharine Streeper, 446.
Margaret Streeper, 447.
Martha A. Streeper, 448.
Elizabeth Streeper, 449.
Isabella Swartz, 738.
Margaret Swartz, 739.
Jane Swartz, 740.
Martha Eliza Sisty, 1214.
John Beans Sisty, 1215.
Mary Amanda Sisty, 1216.
Anna Augusta Sisty, 1217.

Banner Taylor, 260.
Watson W. Taylor, 261.
Seriphine Taylor, 262.
Mary Taylor, 263.
Joseph C. Terry, 103.
Martha Terry, 104.
James Terry, 105.
Harvey Terry, 406.
Isaiah B. Terry, 407.
Eliza Jane Terry, 408.
Hannah A. Terry, 409.
John V. Terry, 410.
Mary Ann Terry, 411.
Oliver Terry, 412.
Caroline Terry, 413.
Jonathan Vansant Terry, 418.
Martha Terry, 419.
William Terry, 420.
Samuel B. Terry, 421.
James M. Terry, 422.
Alitha W. Terry, 423.
Edward Terry, 424.
Wesley B. Terry, 425.
Mary V. Terry, 426.
Rachel Ann Terry, 427.
Ruth Terry, 428.
Sarah A. Terry, 429.
Margaret Emma Terry, 430.
Isaac Kline Terry, 431.
Joseph Carver Terry, 432.
Sarah J. Terry, 1104.
Maranda Terry, 1105, 1184.
Sarah Jane Terry, 1183.
Walter Evans Terry, 1195.
J. Herman Terry, 1196.
John Watson Terry, 1197.
Harvey B. Terry, 1198.
Catharine Terry, 1199.
Annie Terry, 1200.
Oliver T. Terry, 1201.
Wm. Terry, 1218.
Robert B. Terry, 1219.
Alonzo Terry, 1220.
Frank Terry, 1221.
Annie Terry, 1225.
Margaret Terry, 1226, 1278.
William Terry, 1227.
Elizabeth Terry, 1228, 1277.
Sarah Terry, 1229.
Laura Terry, 1230.
John Terry, 1231.
Franklin Terry, 1279.
Miles Terry, 1280.
Thomas Terry, 1281.
Alma Terry, 1282.

Henry M. Torbert, 990.
Maria V. Torbert, 991.
Margaret Torbert, 992.
Alfred Torbert, 993.
Wilson Trego, 1085.
Watson D. Trego, 1086.
Mary E. Trego, 1087.
Rosa Ella Trego, 1958.
Edith L. Trego, 1959.
Edgar B. Trego, 1960.
Mary B. Trego, 1961.
Abby B. Trego, 1962.
Allen W. Trego, 1963.
Nellie W. Trego, 1964.

Harrold Trader, 1651.
Kitty Castle Trader, 1652.
Howard Thompson, 1941.
Mary Thompson, 1942.
Joseph Twining, 1928.
Harriet S. Tomlinson, 1595.
Wilmer Tomlinson, 1596.
Martha W. Tomlinson, 1597.
Mary Emma Tomlinson, 1598.
John C. Tomlinson, 1599.
Lucy C. Tomlinson, 1600.
Ida M. Tomlinson, 1601.
Herbert Tomlinson, 1602.
Charles Tomlinson, 1603.
Rosa Nellie Ulam, 1965.
Vandegrift John, 2049.
William Wilkinson, 34.
Elizabeth Wilkinson, 35.
John Wilkinson, 36.
Joseph Wilkinson, 37.
Thomas Wilkinson, 38.
Asa Wilkinson, 39.

Anna Eliza Wanamaker, 481.
Letitia Wanamaker, 482.
Mary G. Wanamaker, 483.
Thomas C. Wanamaker, 484.
John E. Wanamaker, 485.
Anna U. Wanamaker, 486.
Alfred Wanamaker, 487.
Henry C. Wanamaker, 488.
Edward Wanamaker, 1377.
Charlotte M. Wanamaker, 1378.
Jennie Wanamaker, 1379.
Elizabeth C. Wanamaker, 1380.
Mary C. Wanamaker, 1381.
Jennie S. Wanamaker, 1382.
Sadie F. Wanamaker, 1383.

Harriet Walton, 381.
John Walton, 382.
Amy Walton, 383.
Watson W. Walton, 921.

William C. Walton, 922.
Rachel K. Walton, 923.
Laura K. Walton, 924.
Louisa M. Walton, 925.
Arrita D. Walton, 1457.
Emma Augustus Walton, 1574.
Josephine E. Walton, 1575.
Horace Man Walton, 1576.
Martha Evans Walton, 1577.
Lucius Leedom Walton, 1578.

—— Wambold, son, 1870.
—— Wambold, son, 1880.
Chas. H. Warner, 1089.
Andrew Ward, 1125.
Watson T. Ward, 1126.
Emily Ann Ward, 1127.
Phebe C. Ward, 1128.
Amos Addis Ward, 1129.
Alfred R. Ward, 1976.
John Ward, 1977.
Gertrude Ward, 1978.
Anna J. Ward, 1979.
Ella D. Ward, 1980.
George H. Ward, 1981.
Harry H. Ward, 1982.
Lizzie B. Ward, 1983.
William H. Watson, 1414.
Thos. Wesley Watson, 1415.
Emma Florance Watson, 1416.
Narcissa Watson, 1417.
Alfred C. Watson, 1418.

Anna Williams, 1047.
Henry Williams, 1048, 1943.
Chas. F. Williams, 1049.
Mary C. Williams, 1050.
Annie Williams, 1051.
George M. Williams, 1944.
Carrie Williams, 1945.
Julias Wilson, 1445.
Caroline Wilson, 1446.

Maria White, 657.
David White, 658.
Mary A. White, 659.
Sarah White, 660.
Elizabeth White, 661.
Israel White, 662.
Lama White, 728.
—— White, 729.

Iris C. Wood, 1532.
Jane C. Wood, 1533.
Jonathan B. Wood, 1534.
Isaac B. Wood, 1535.

Henry M. Wood, 1536.
Heil Wood, 1537.
Sophia Wood, 1538.
Cynthia E. Wood, 1539.
Winfield S. Wood, 1541.
Catharine E. Wood, 1540.
John Wood, 1232.
Aletha Wood, 1233.
Albert Woodman, 1900.
Paul Woodman, 1901.
Grace Woodman, 1902.
George Wiley, 1467.

William Worthington, 40.
Amos Worthington, 41.
Heber Worthington, 42.
Joseph Worthington, 43.
John Worthington, 44.
Elizabeth Worthington, 45.
Mary Worthington, 46.
Spencer T. Worthington, 790.
Martha Worthington, 791.
Martha C. Worthington, 1090.
John J. Worthington, 1091.
Mary Ellen Worthington, 1092.
Keziah Worthington, 1093.
Sarah M. Worthington, 1094.
Silas Worthington, 1095.
Henry Worthington, 1096.
Edward Worthington, 1097.
Cynthia Worthington, 1098.
Edward R. Worthington, 1447.
Samuel C. Worthington, 1448.
Linford E. Worthington, 1449.
Warran Worthington, 1450.
William C. Woodman, 786.

Samuel C. Wright, 1526.
Euphemia A. Wright, 1527.
Elmer E. Wright, 1528.
George B. Wright, 1529.
Alfred E. Wright, 1530.

William Yates, 1106.
Mary Yates, 1107.
Elizabeth Yates, 1108.
Edith Yates, 1109.
Isabella Yates, 1110.
Margaret Yates, 1111.
Edward Yates, 1112.
Laura Yates, 1113.
Ella Yates, 1114.
Maggie Yerkes, 1917.
John Yerkes, 1918.

Made in the USA
Columbia, SC
04 February 2019